Parry Sound Ontario in Colour Photos, Saving Our History One Photo at a Time

Photography
by Barbara Raué
©2022

Series Name: Cruising Ontario

Book 217: Parry Sound

Cover photo: 72 Gibson Street, Page 32

©All the photos in this book have been taken with my cameras. I own the rights to them.

Series Name: Cruising Ontario
Saving Our History One Photo at a Time
in colour photos

Books Available in Alphabetical Order:
Aberfoyle, Acton, Ajax, Alton, Amherstburg, Ancaster, Arthur, Auburn, Aylmer, Ayr, Beaver Valley, Belgrave, Belleville, Bloomingdale, Blyth, Brantford, Brockville, Burford, Burlington, Caledon, Caledonia, Cambridge, Carlow, Chatsworth, Clifford, Collingwood, Conestogo, Delhi, Dorchester to Aylmer, Drayton, Drumbo, Dundas, Dunlop, Eden Mills, Elmira, Elora, Erin, Essex, Fergus, Goderich, Grimsby, Guelph, Hagersville, Hamilton, Hanover, Harriston, Hespeler, Jarvis, Kingston, Kingsville, Kitchener, Lake Superior, Lincoln, Linwood, Listowel, London, Lucknow, Merrickville, Mono, Mount Forest, Mount Pleasant, Neustadt, New Hamburg, Newboro, Newport, Niagara-on-the-Lake, Niagara Falls, North Bay, Oakville, Onondaga, Orangeville, Orillia, Oshawa, Owen Sound, Palmerston, Paris, Pelham, Perth, Peterborough, Petrolia, Pickering, Port Colborne, Port Elgin, Portland, Preston, Rockwood, Sarnia, Sault Ste. Marie, Seaforth, Sheffield, Shelburne, Simcoe, Smiths Falls, Smithville, Southampton, St. Catharines, St. George, St. Jacobs, St. Marys, St. Thomas, Stoney Creek, Stratford, Thamesford, Thunder Bay, Tillsonburg, Toronto, Waterdown, Waterford, Waterloo, Welland, Wellesley, West Flamborough, Westport, Whitby, Windsor, Wingham, Woodstock

Book 210: North Bay
Book 211: Fort Erie
Book 212-215: Haldimand
    County
Book 216: Sudbury
Book 217: Parry Sound

Table of Contents

Dunchurch	Page 5
Avenue Road	Page 6
Waubeek Street	Page 8
Seguin Street	Page 11
North Tudhope Street	Page 16
James Street	Page 16
Belvedere Avenue	Page 24
Ashwood Drive	Page 28
Gibson Street	Page 29
Church Street	Page 37
McMurray Street	Page 49
Mary Street	Page 51
Bay Street	Page 56
Scenic Lookout Tower	Page 60
Cascade Street	Page 66

Parry Sound is a located in northern Ontario on the eastern shore of Parry Sound. It is 160 kilometres (99 miles) south of Sudbury and 225 kilometres (140 miles) north of Toronto. It is a popular cottage country region. It has the world's deepest natural freshwater port.

Muskoka District was named after an Indian Chief, probably Misquuckkey of the Chippawas, who until the treaty of 1815 was lord of this Venetian district of Ontario. While the heavy pine and hardwood forests were still in their primeval beauty, many people including Government agents considered the country was fit for settlement. In 1859 the first land grants were made.

About 1857 James and William Gibson erected a sawmill at the mouth of the Seguin River. William Beatty, with his sons James and William, acquired the mill in 1863, and the following year were granted a licence of occupation for two thousand acres. In addition to lumbering, they laid out a town plot, promoted settlement, opened a store, built a church, constructed roads, and operated boats on Lake Huron and a stage service to Bracebridge. William "Governor" Beatty (1835-1898) lived here and managed the family's enterprises which stimulated the growth of Parry Sound. Incorporated as a town in 1887, it was named in honour of Sir William Edward Parry, noted Arctic explorer.

During the early part of the 20th century, the area was a popular subject for the many scenic art works of Tom Thomson and members of the Group of Seven.

The eastern coast of Georgian Bay where Parry Sound is located is known as the "30,000 Islands" and is considered the world's largest freshwater archipelago. It covers 347,000 hectares of shoreline ecosystem, and over 100 species of animals and plants that are at risk in Canada and Ontario, including unique reptiles and amphibians.

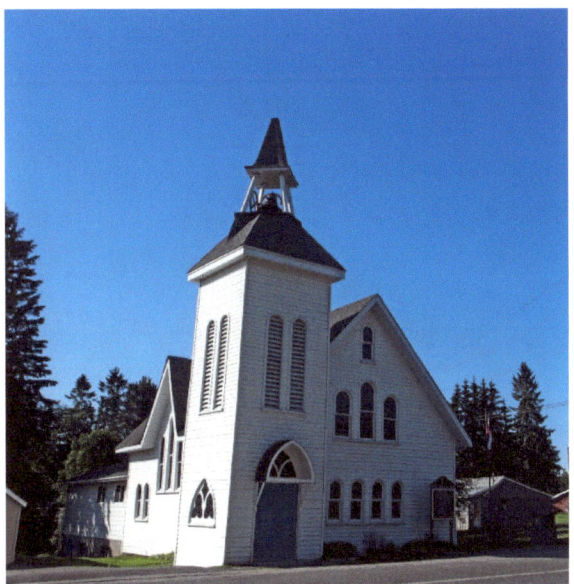
Dunchurch Knox United Church

Dunchurch is a community in Ontario located in the municipality of Whitestone in Parry Sound District.

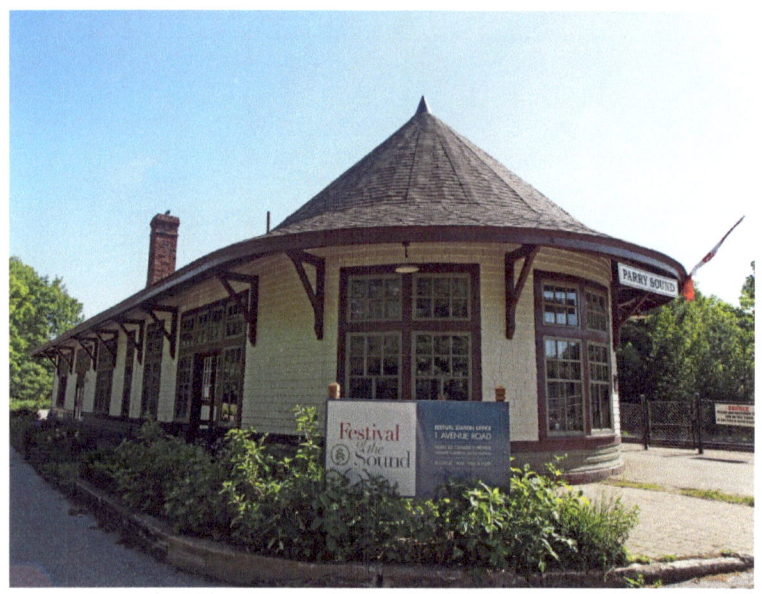

1 Avenue Road - The Canadian Pacific Railway (CPR) built this station in 1907 when it opened a Toronto-Sudbury Branch line. The building is a bold composition of a steep, picturesque roofline with a bellcast canopy, and a large corner tower.

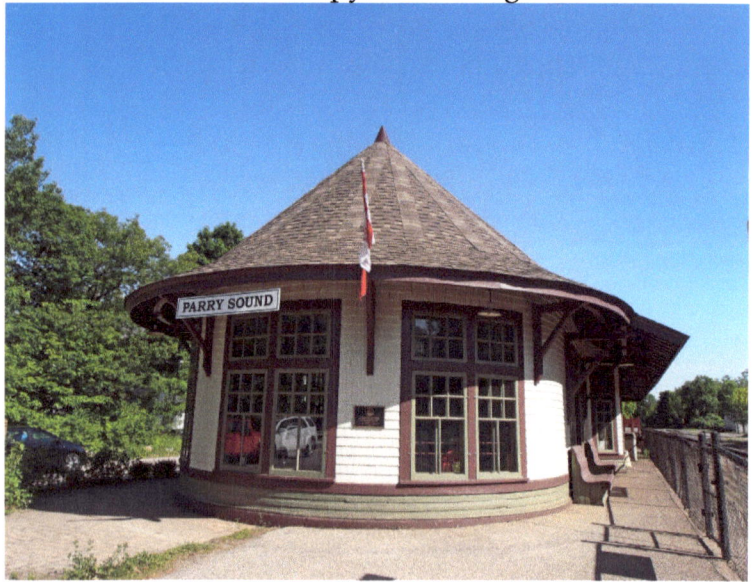

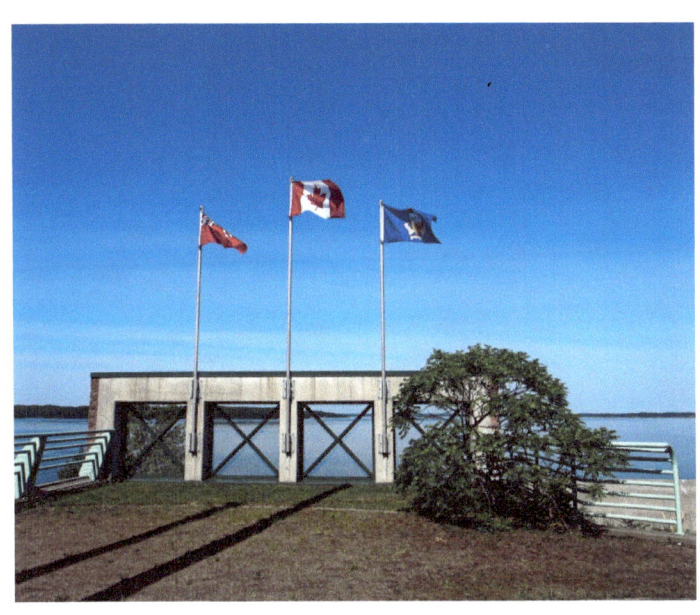

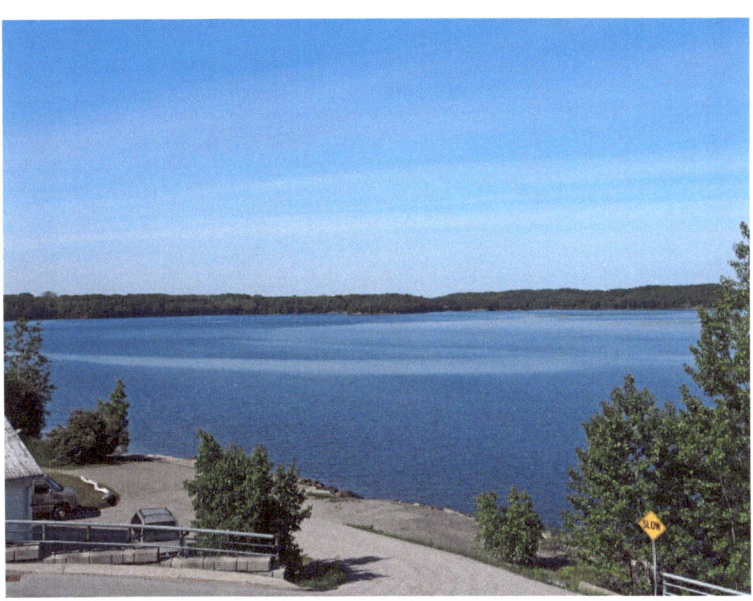

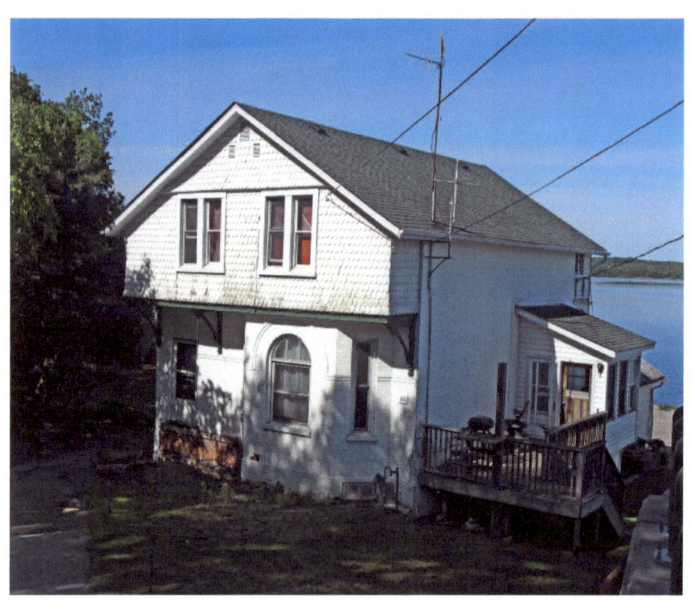

#86

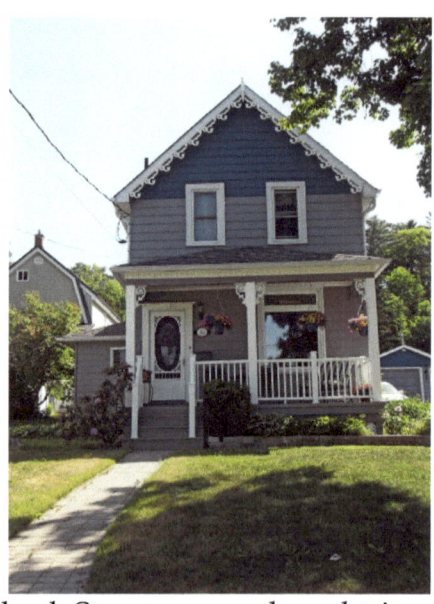

43 Waubeek Street – verge board trim on gable

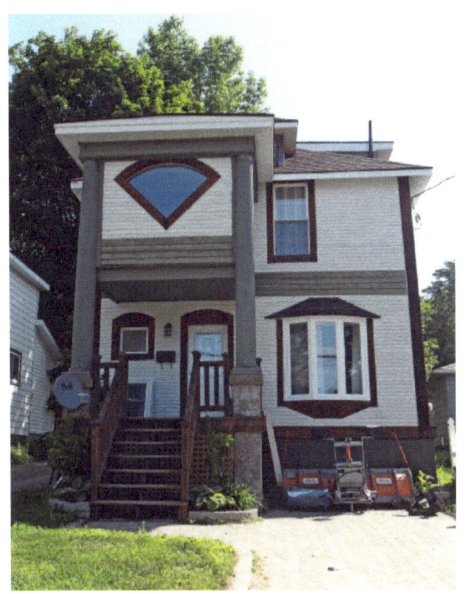

Waubeek Street

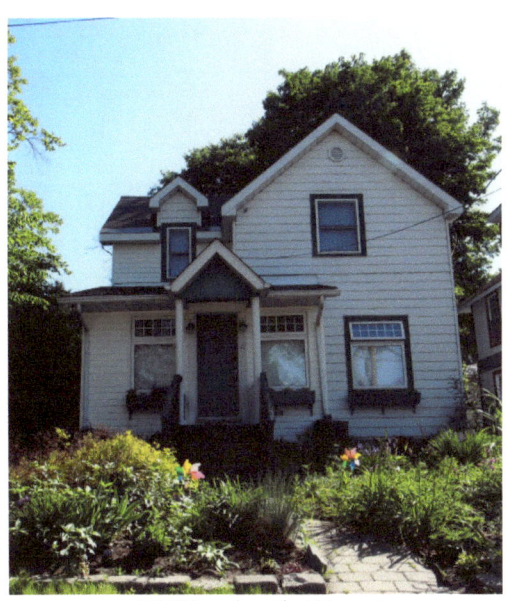

47 Waubeek Street

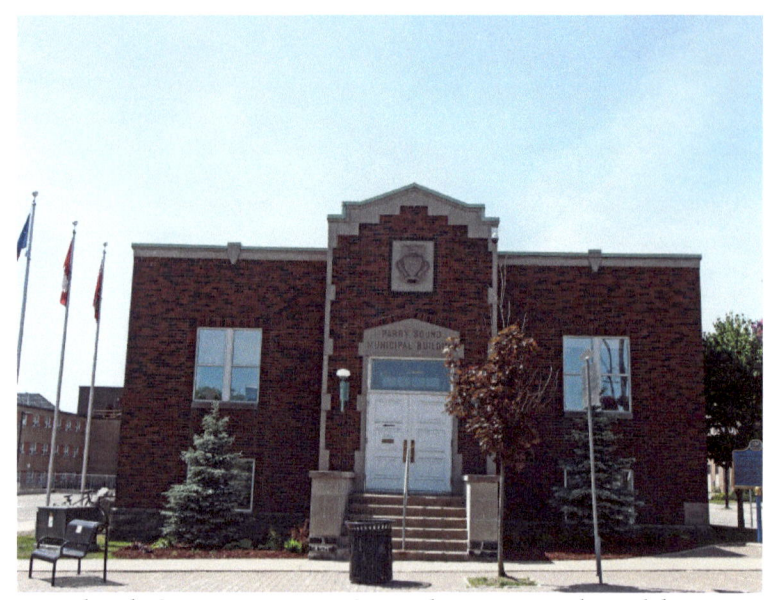

52 Waubeek Street – Parry Sound Municipal Building - 1934

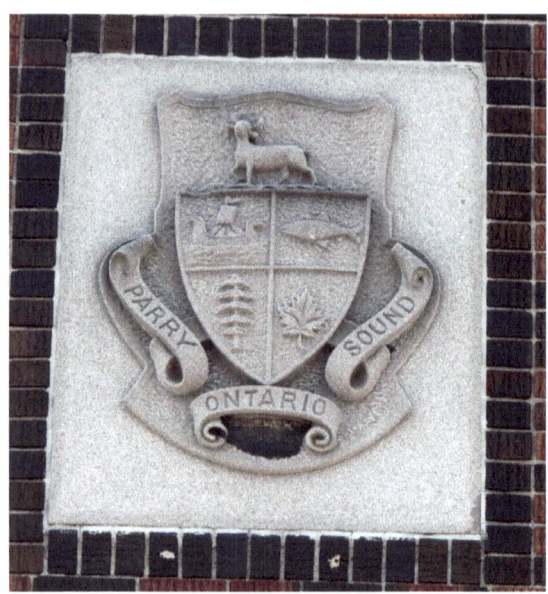

Parry Sound Crest

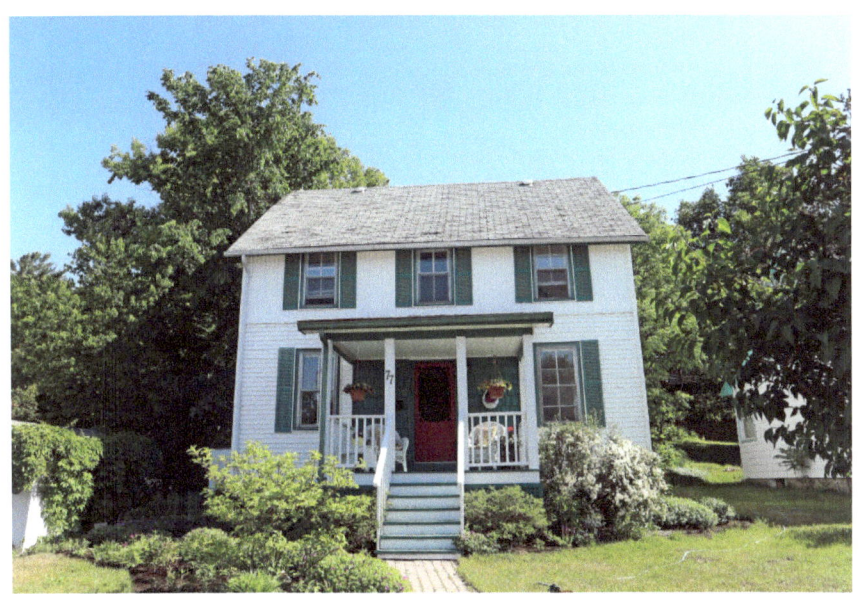

77 Waubeek Street

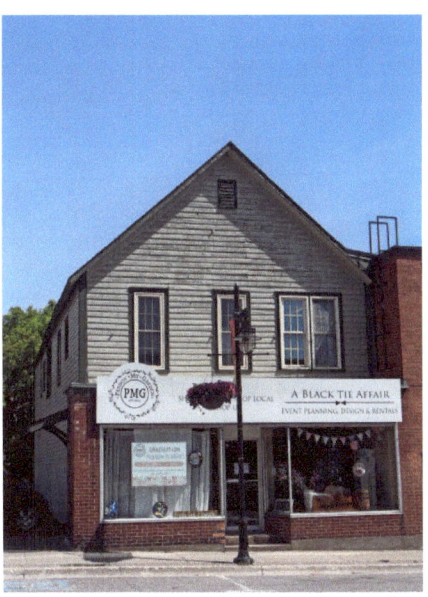

35 Seguin Street – Pardon My Garden florist

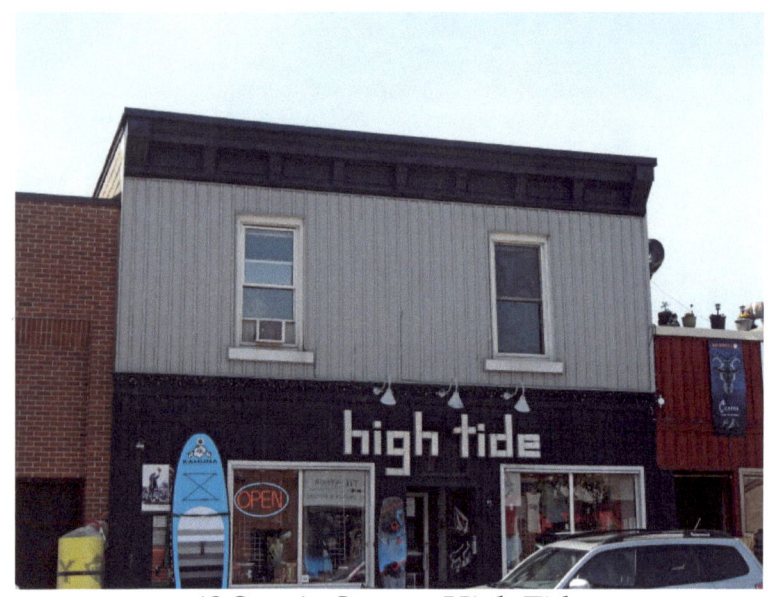

42 Seguin Street – High Tide

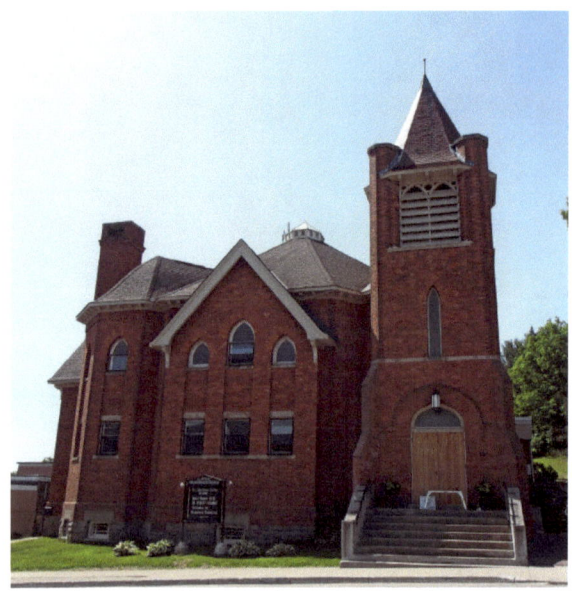

58 Seguin Street – St. Andrew's Presbyterian Church

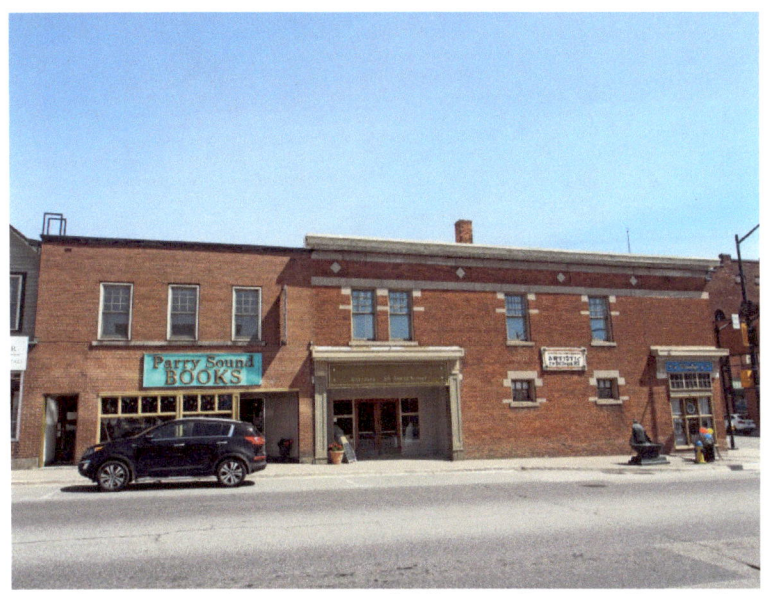

Seguin Street – main entrance 26 James Street – Parry Sound Books

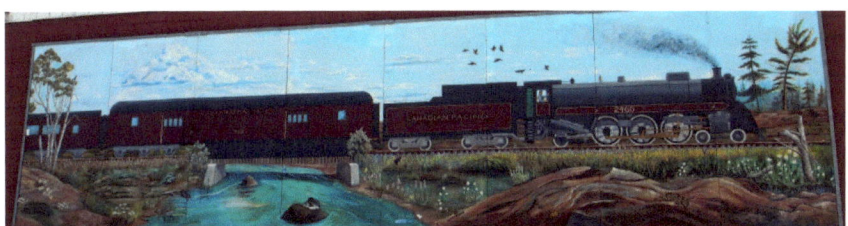

Mural by several artists

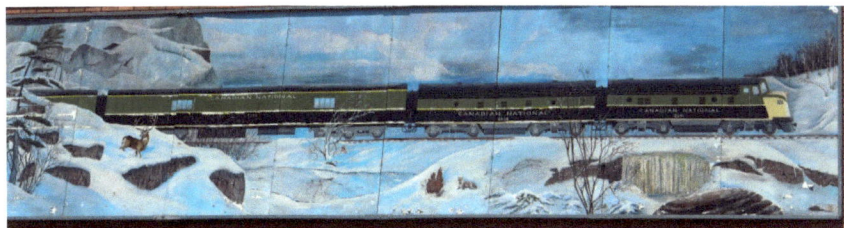

Mural

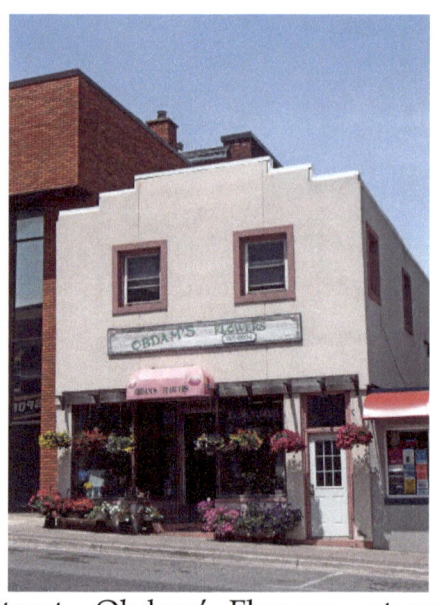

31 Seguin Street – Obdam's Flowers – stepped parapet

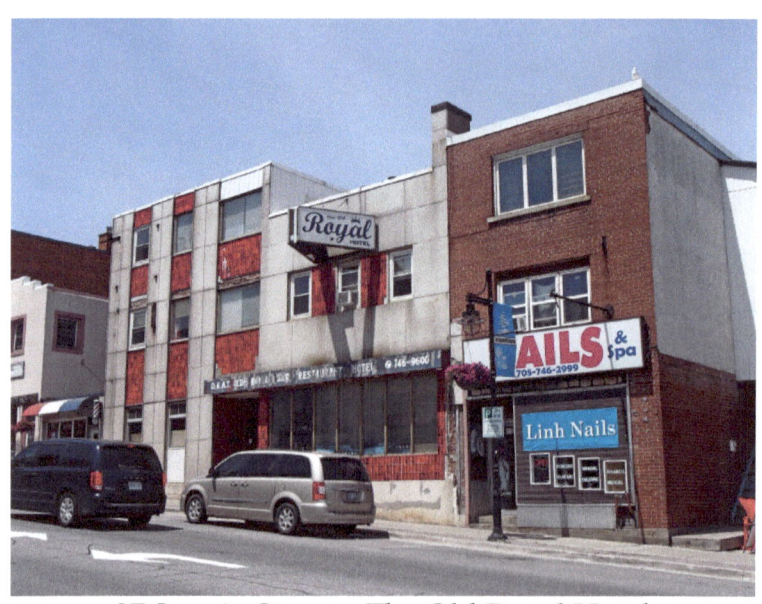

27 Seguin Street – The Old Royal Hotel

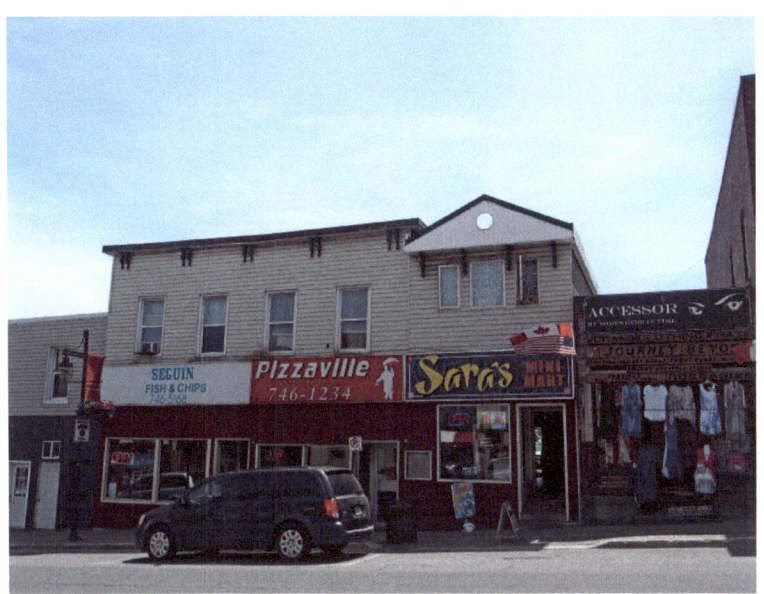

28 Seguin Street – Pizzaville

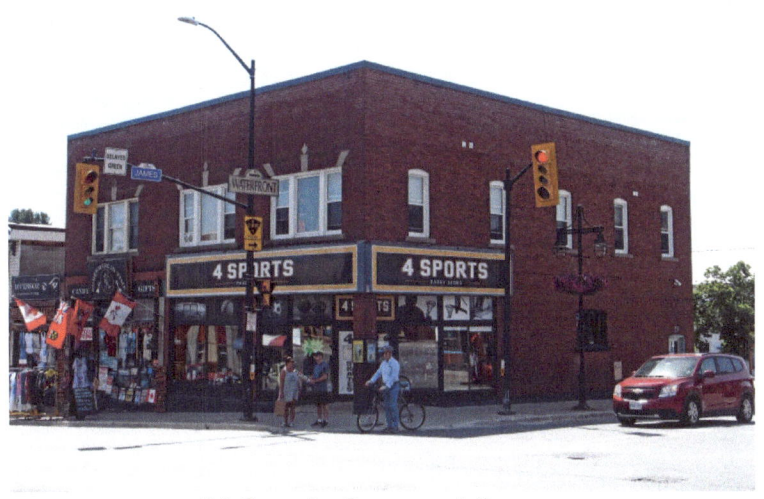

34 Seguin Street – 4 Sports

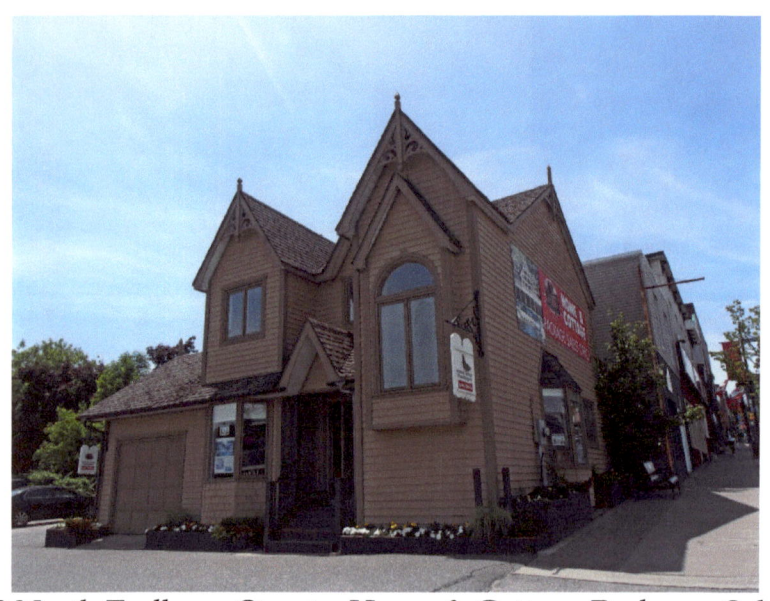

89 North Tudhope Street – Home & Cottage Packages Sales Office

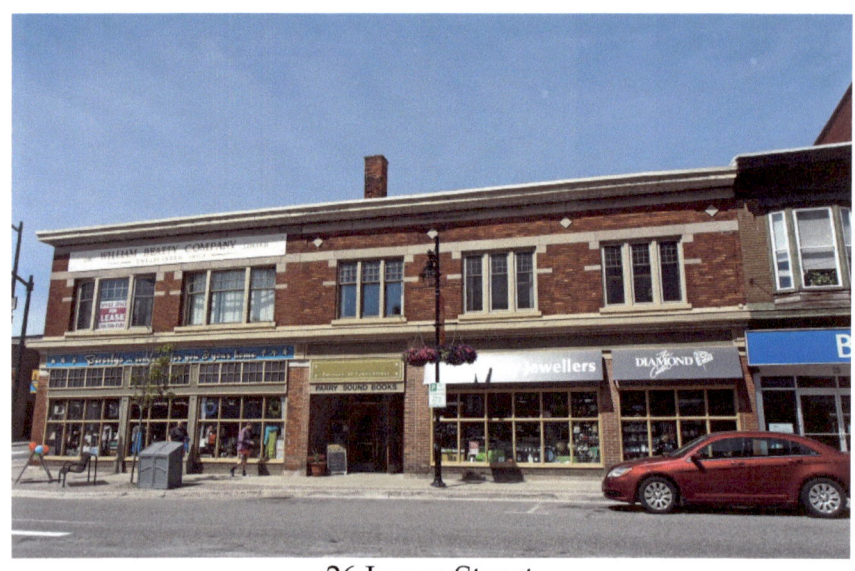

26 James Street

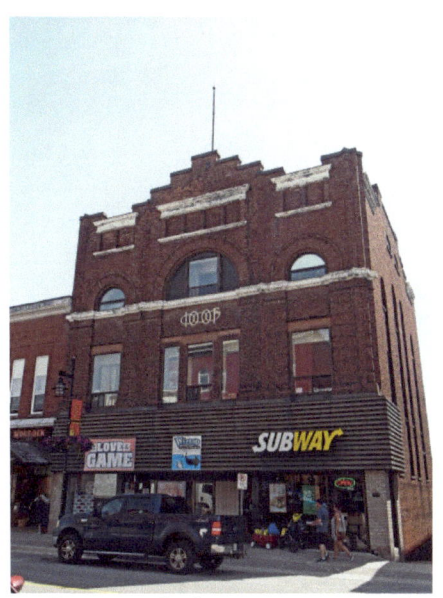

33 James Street – Subway – stepped parapet

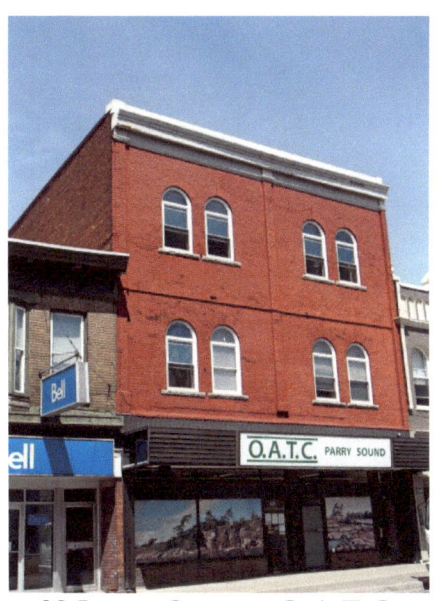

32 James Street – O.A.T.C.

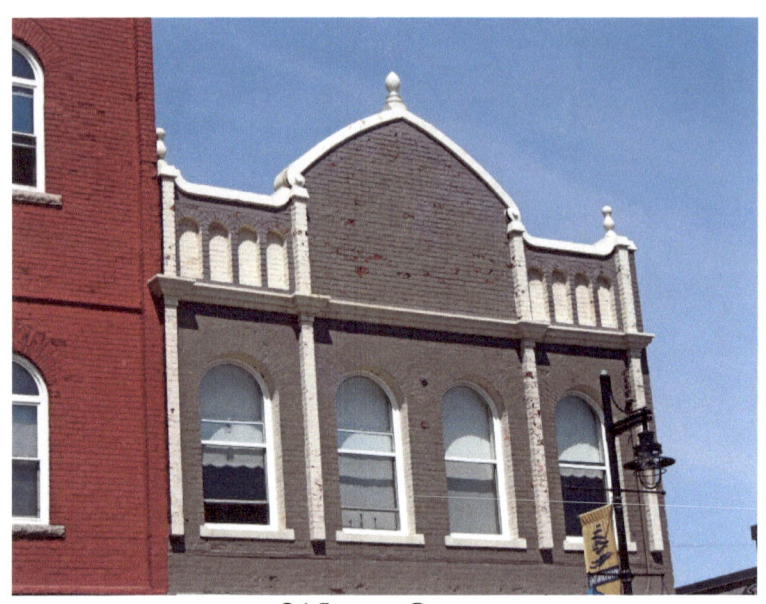

34 James Street

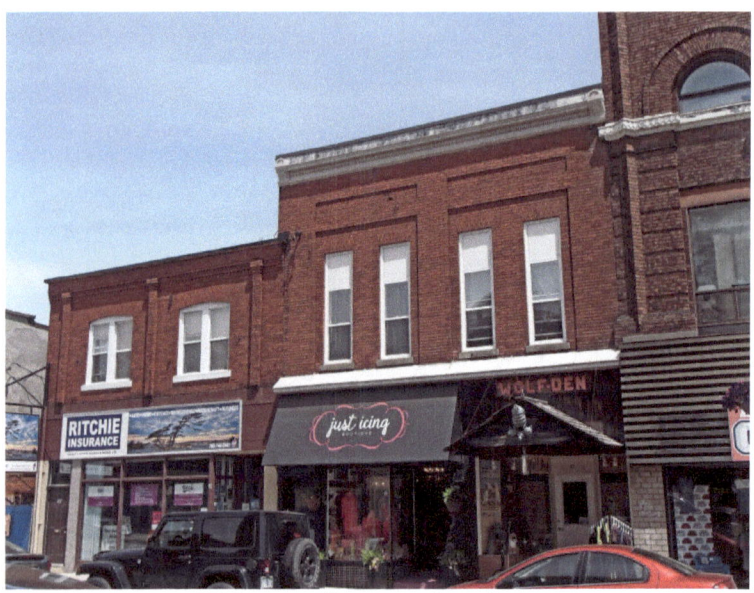

37 James Street – Just Icing

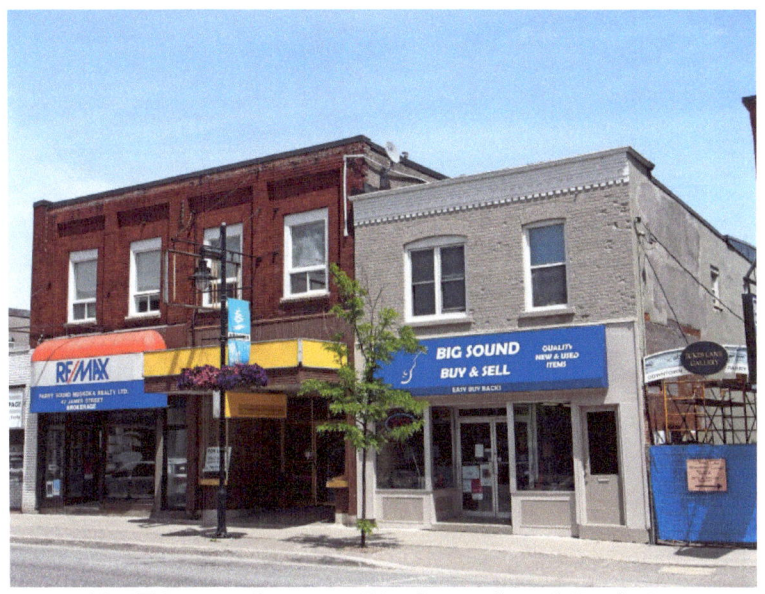

41-47 James Street – Big Sound and Re/Max

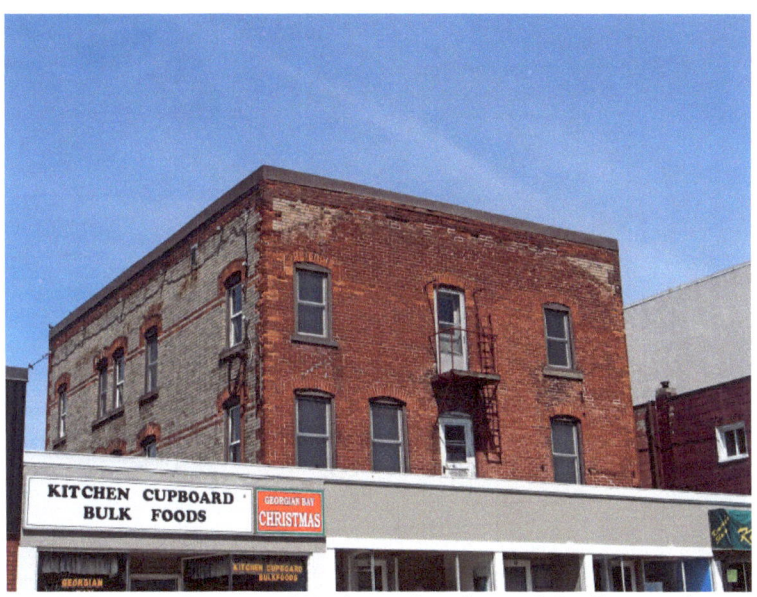

44 James Street – Kitchen Cupboard Bulk Foods

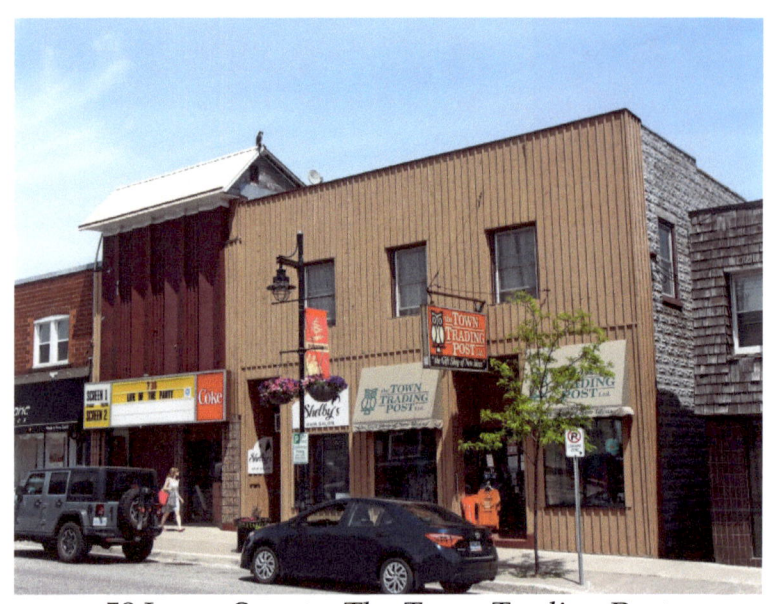

59 James Street – The Town Trading Post

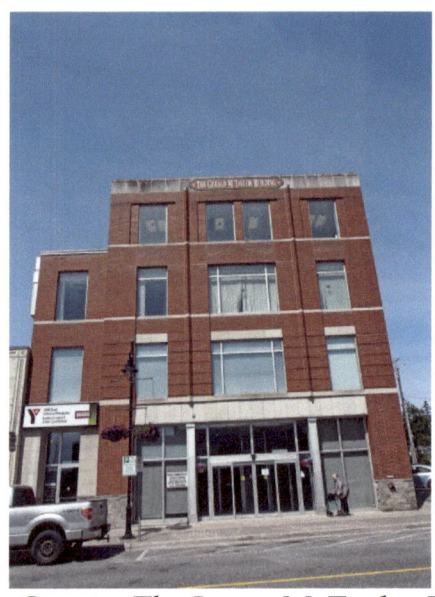

60 James Street – The James M. Taylor Building

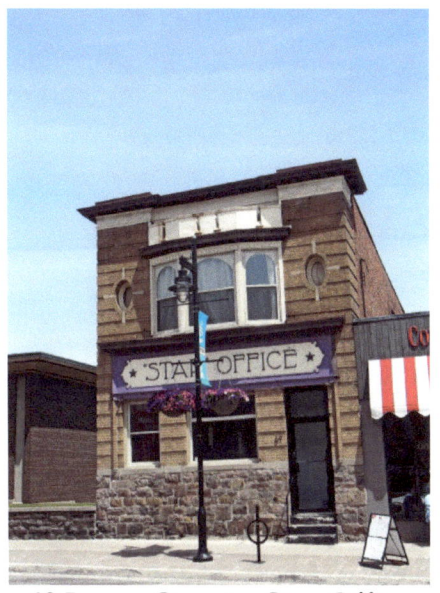

69 James Street – Star Office

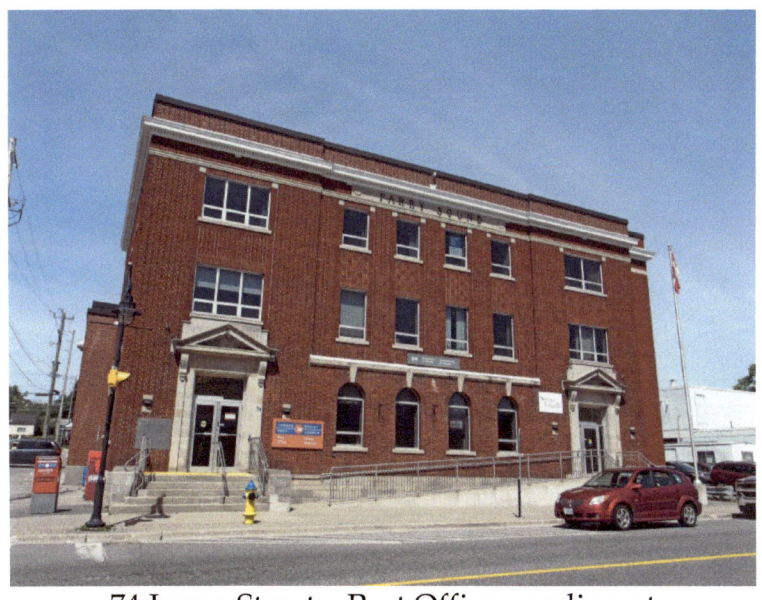

74 James Street – Post Office - pediment

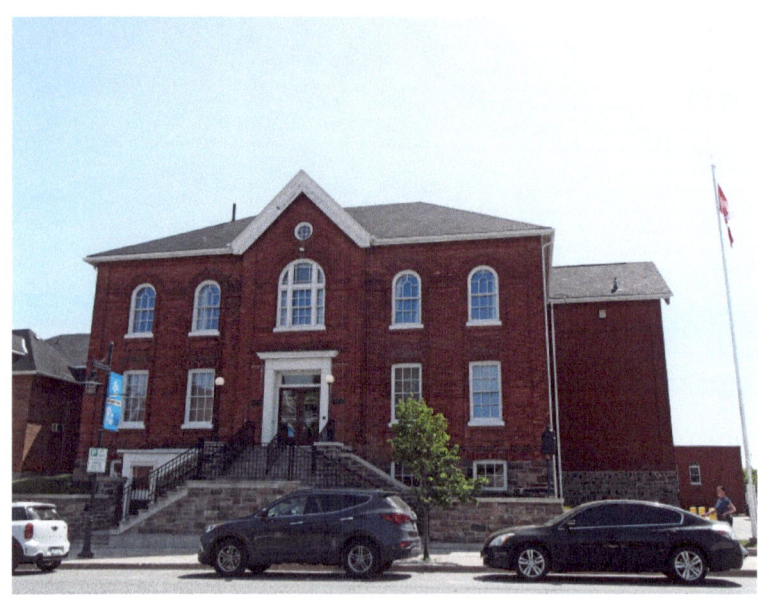

89 James Street – Court House - 1871

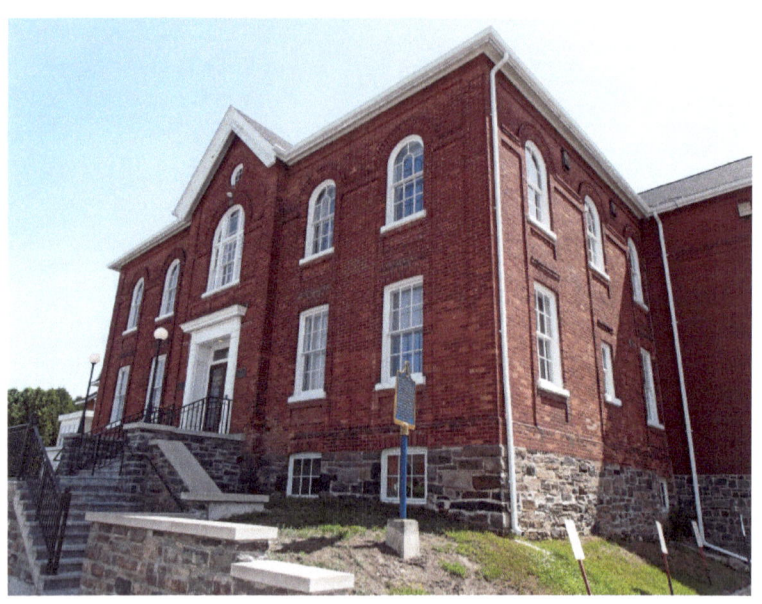

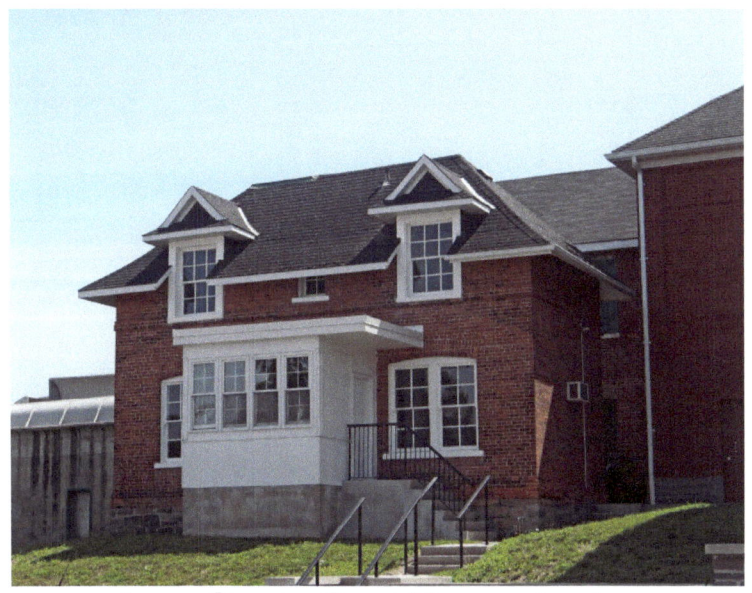

James Street – Court House extension

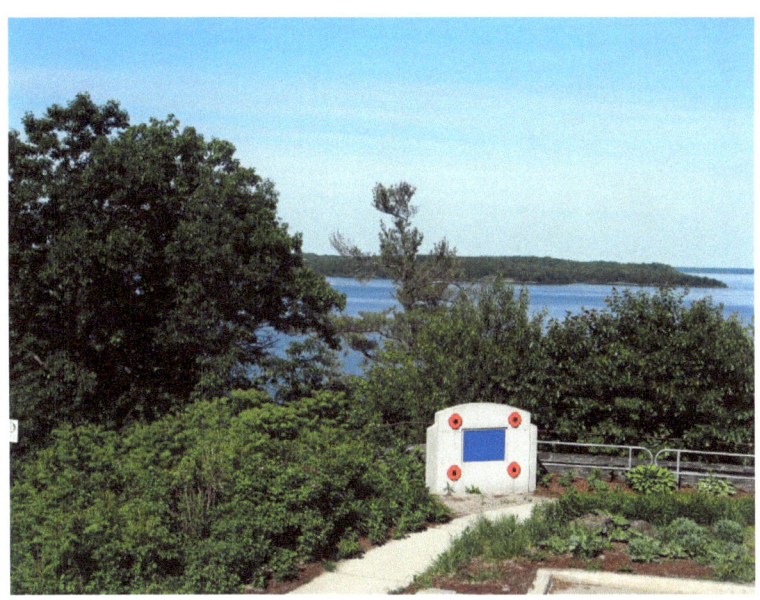

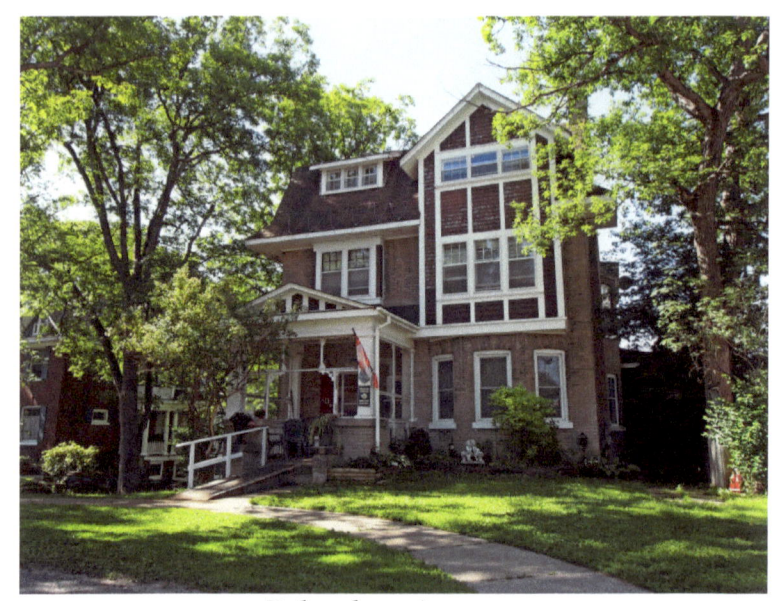

Belvedere Avenue

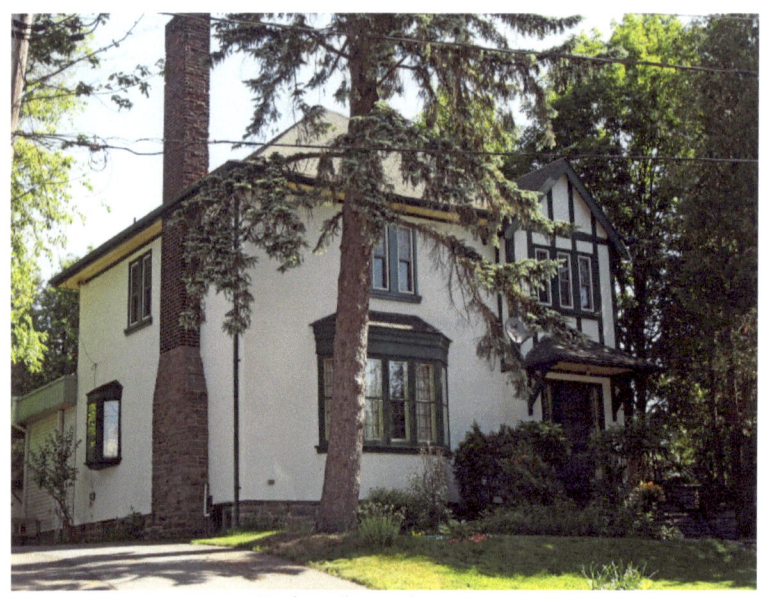

Belvedere Avenue

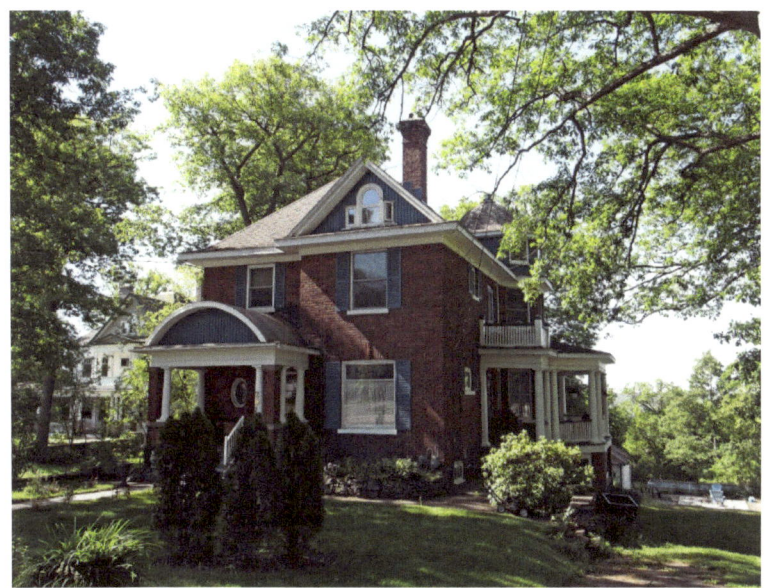

20 Belvedere Avenue – Palladian window in gable, semi-circular pediment

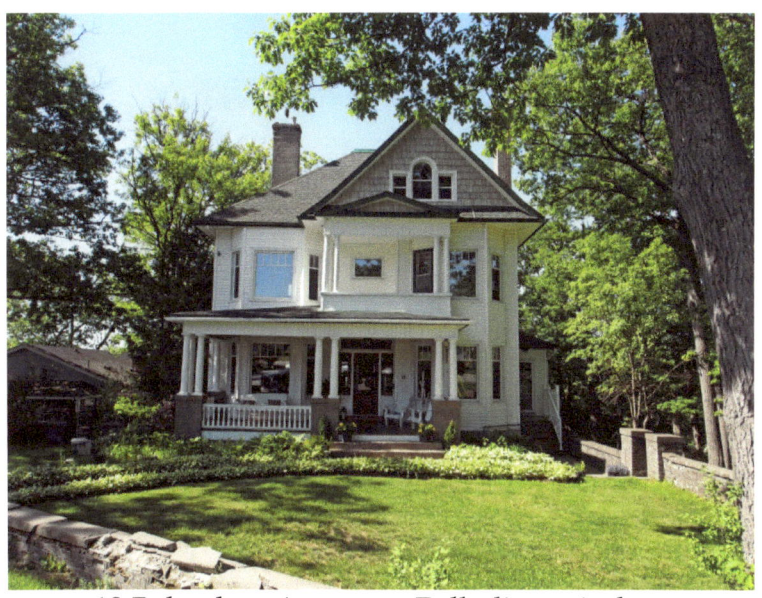

18 Belvedere Avenue – Palladian window

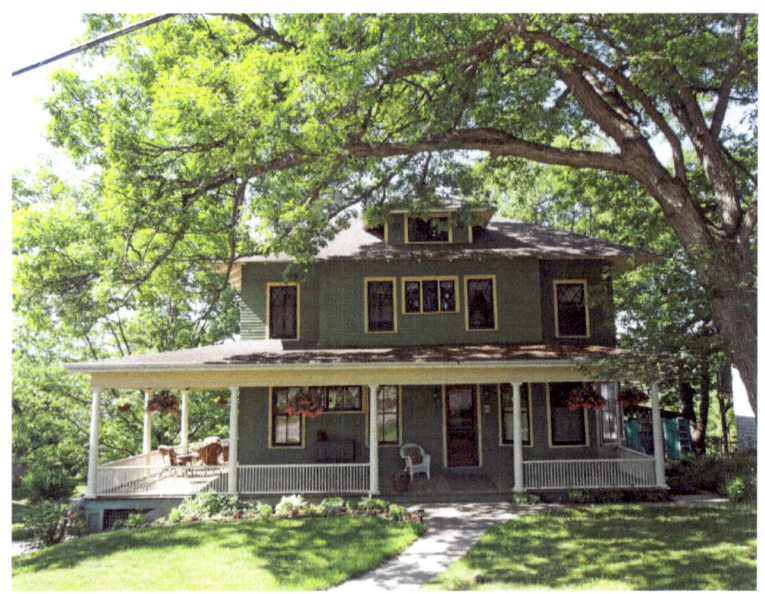

14 Belvedere Avenue – dormer in hipped roof

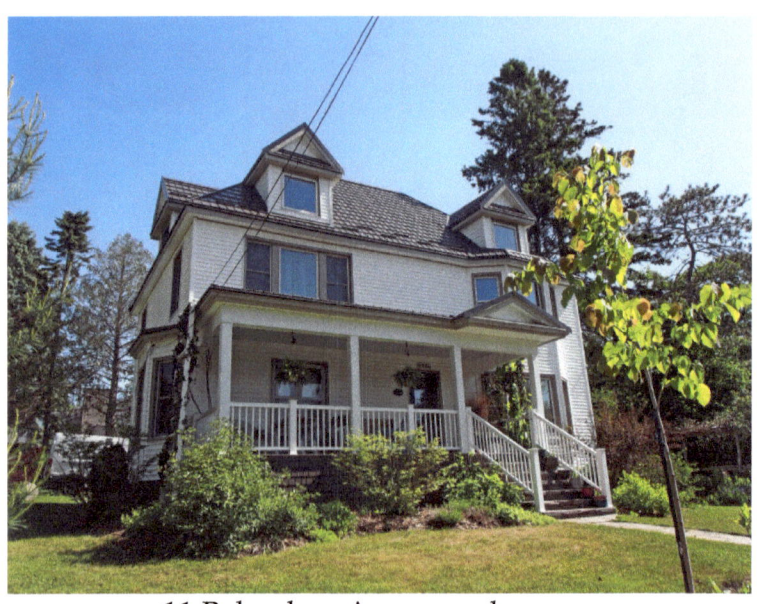

11 Belvedere Avenue - dormers

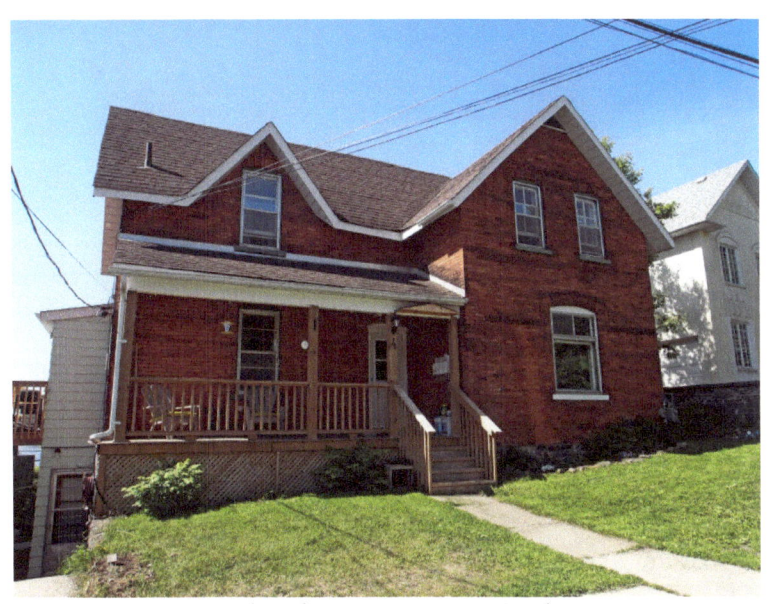

4 Belvedere Avenue - Gothic

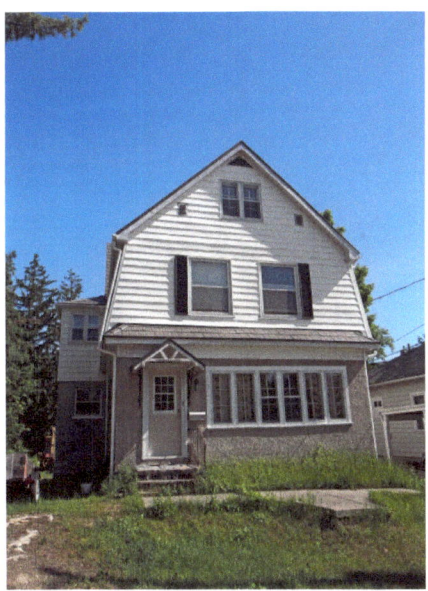

5 Belvedere Avenue

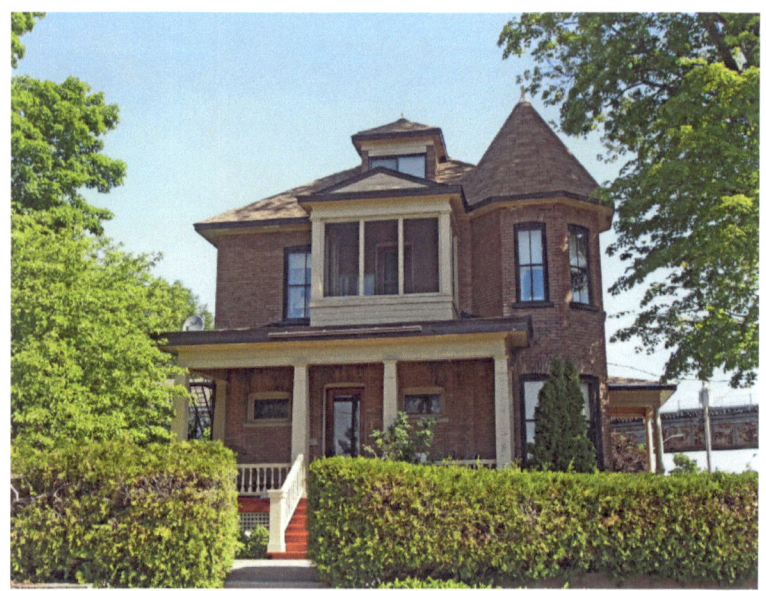

1 Belvedere Avenue – 1907 – turret with cone-shaped roof, dormer

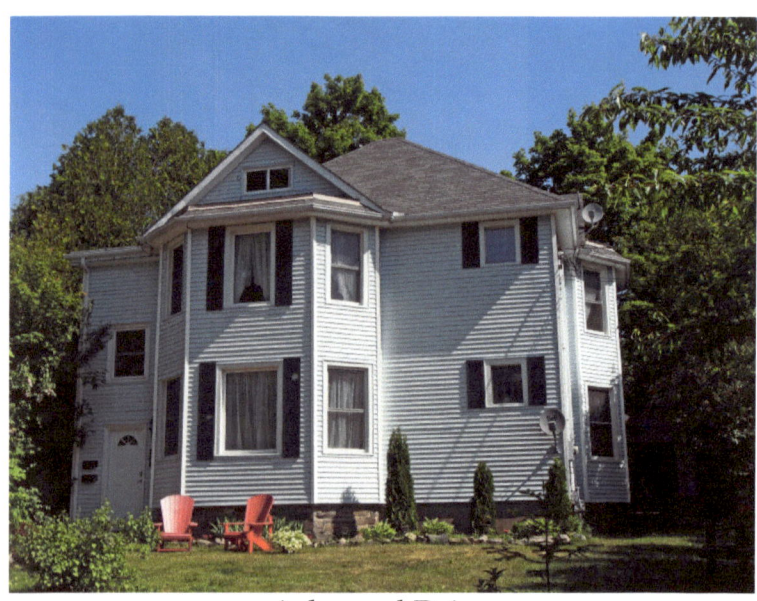

Ashwood Drive

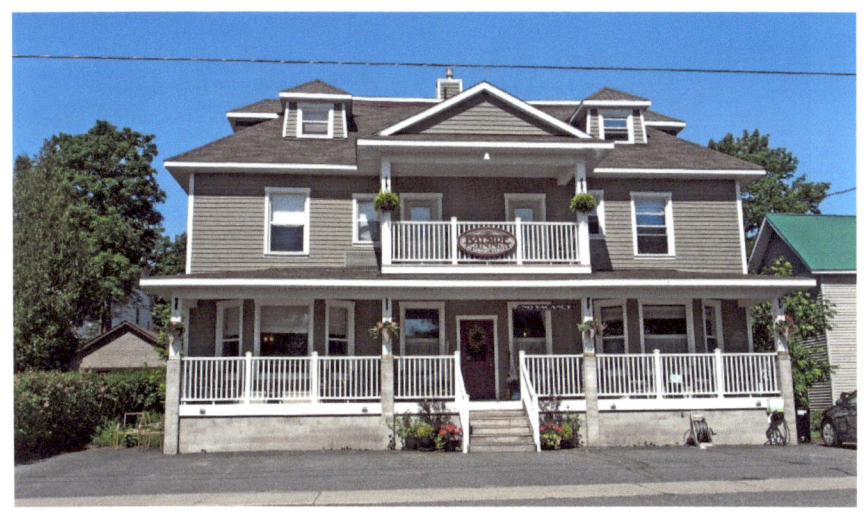

10 Gibson Street – Bayside Inn

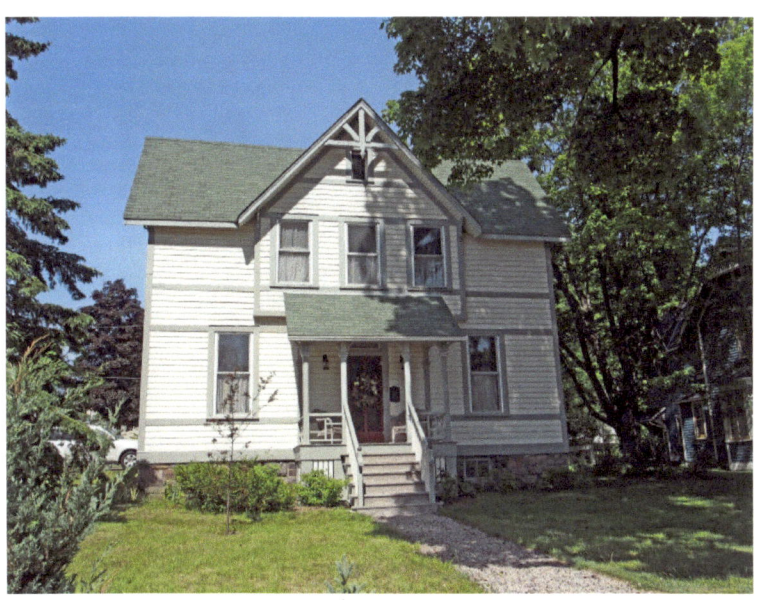

62 Gibson Street

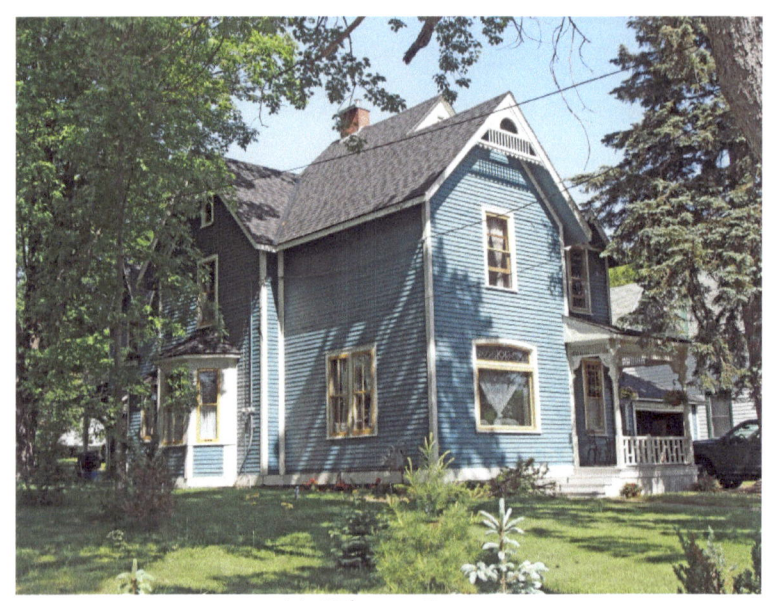

64 Gibson Street

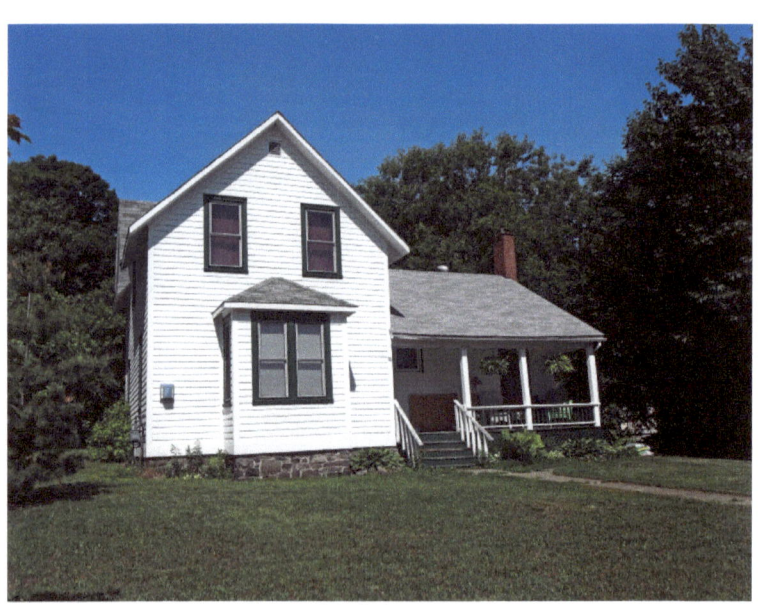

66 Gibson

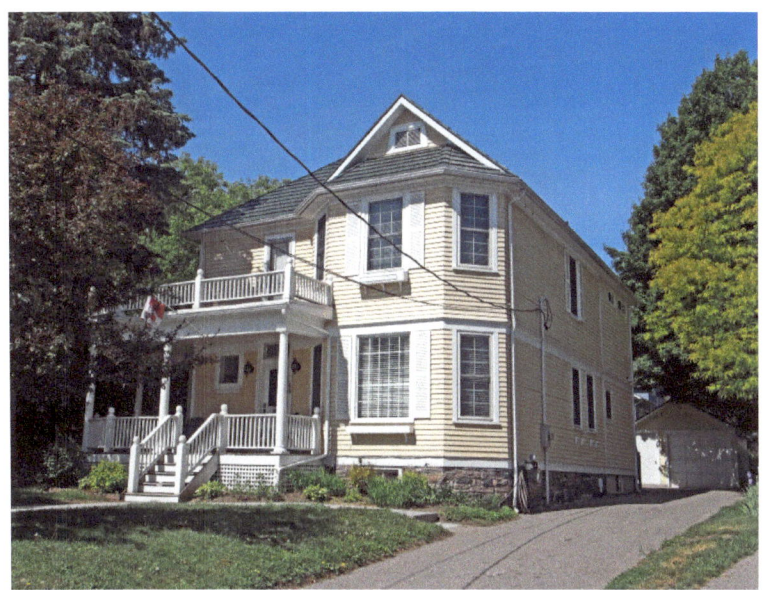

68 Gibson Street

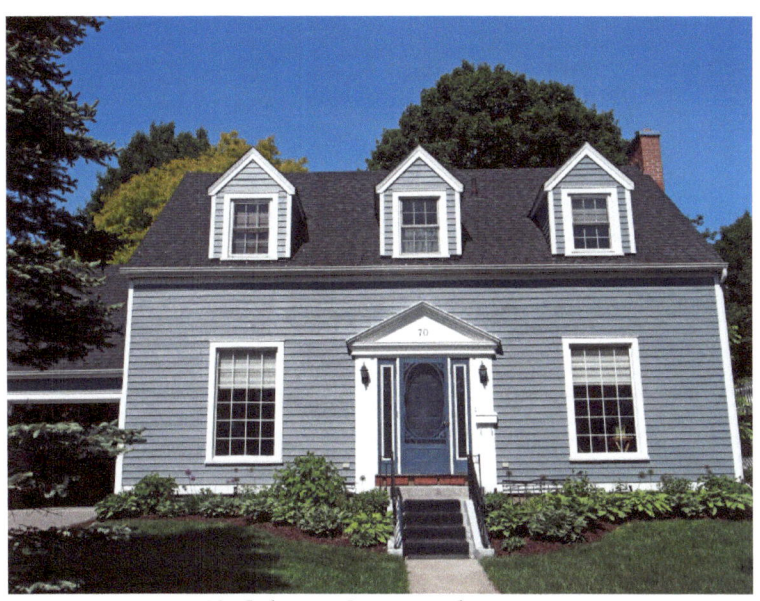

70 Gibson Street - dormers

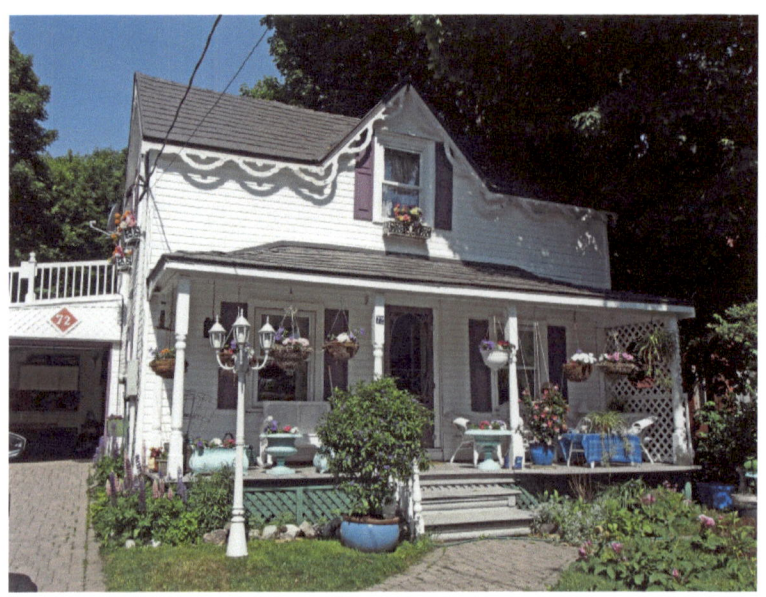

72 Gibson Street – gingerbread trim on gable and roofline

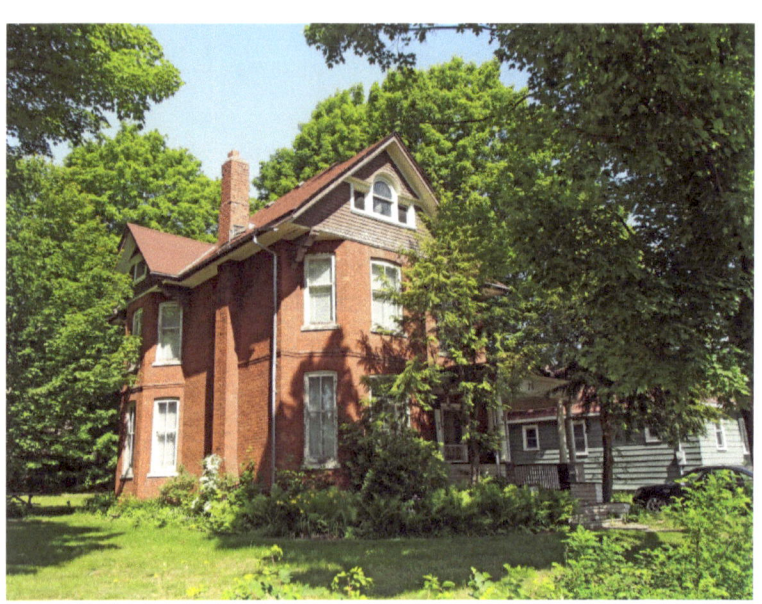

74 Gibson Street – Palladian window in gable

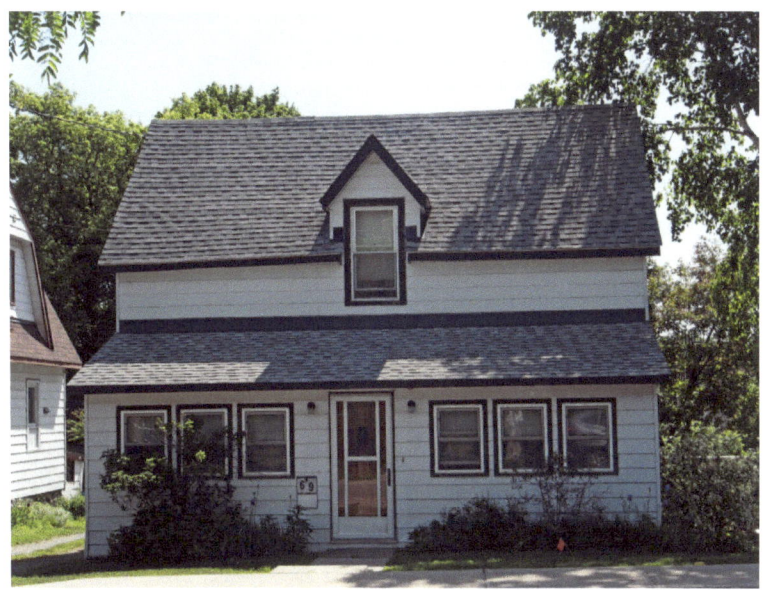

69 Gibson Street - dormer

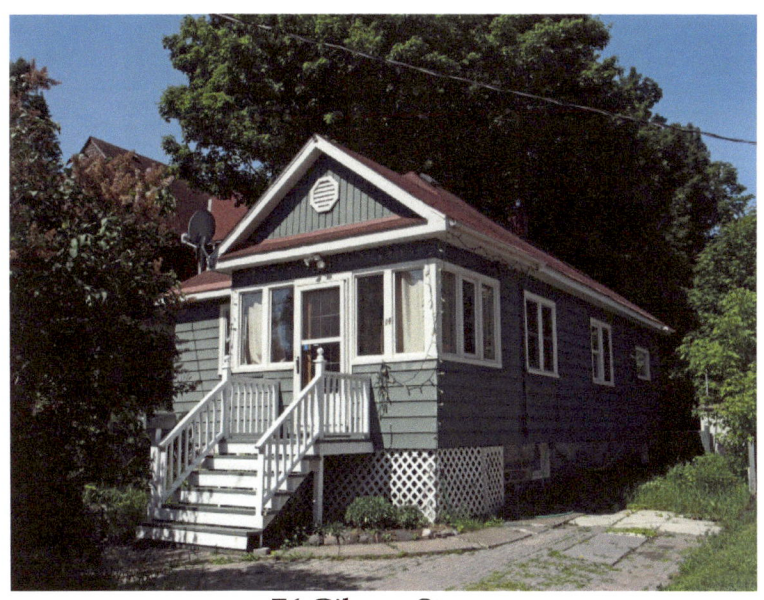

76 Gibson Street

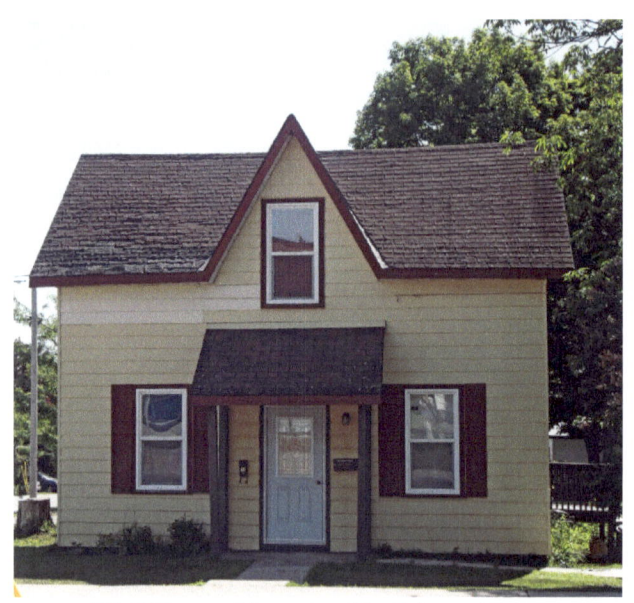

73 Gibson Street – Gothic cottage

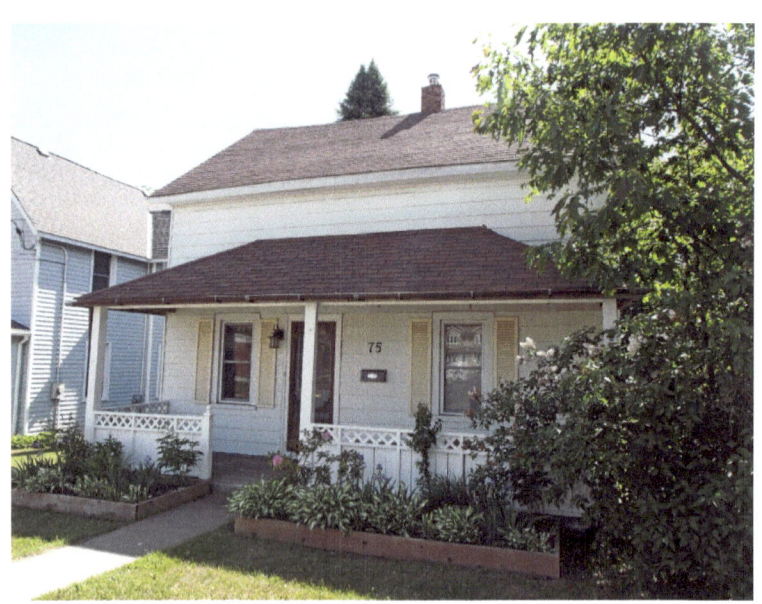

75 Gibson Street

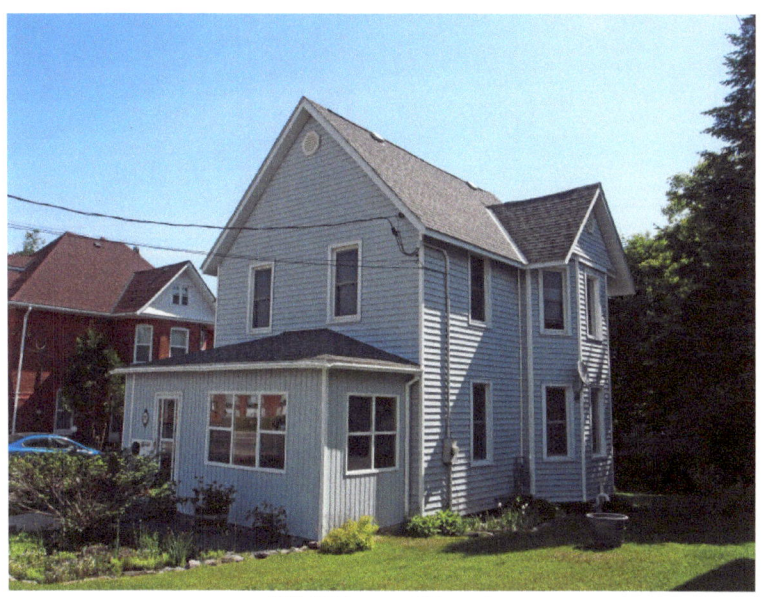

77 Gibson Street

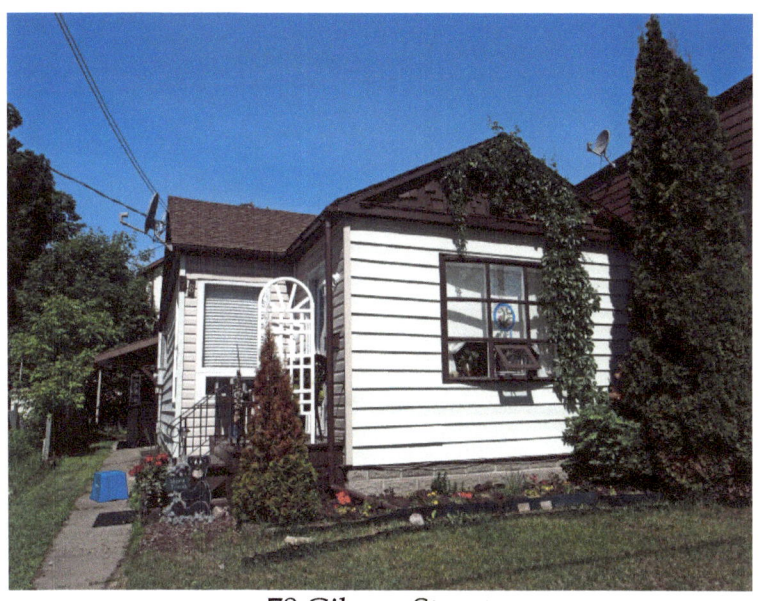

78 Gibson Street

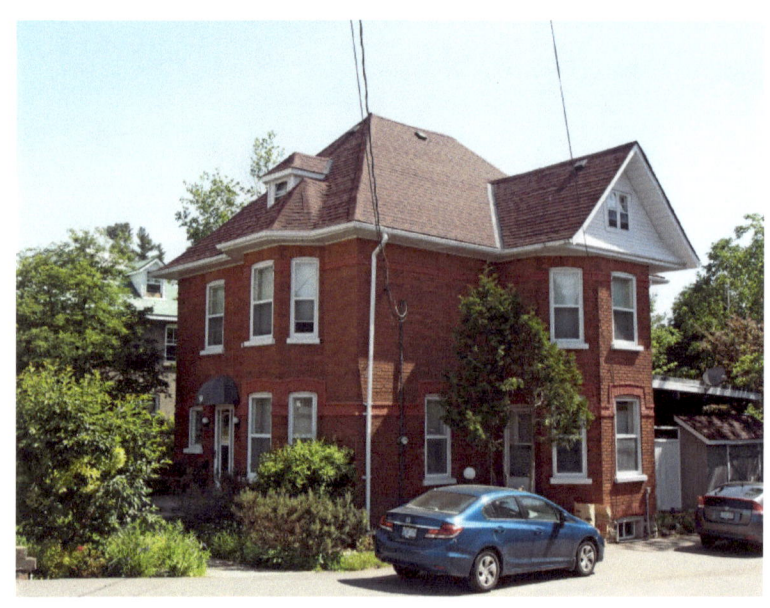

79 Gibson Street

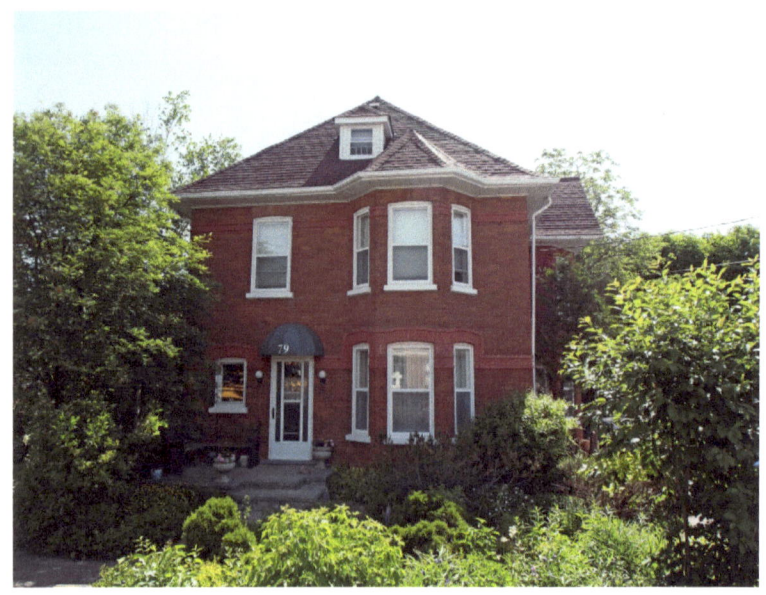

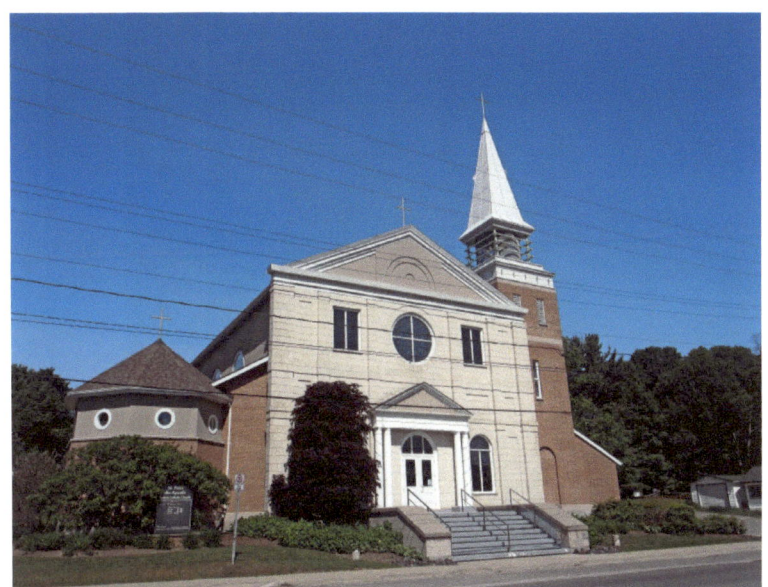

52 Church Street – St. Peter the Apostle Roman Catholic Church

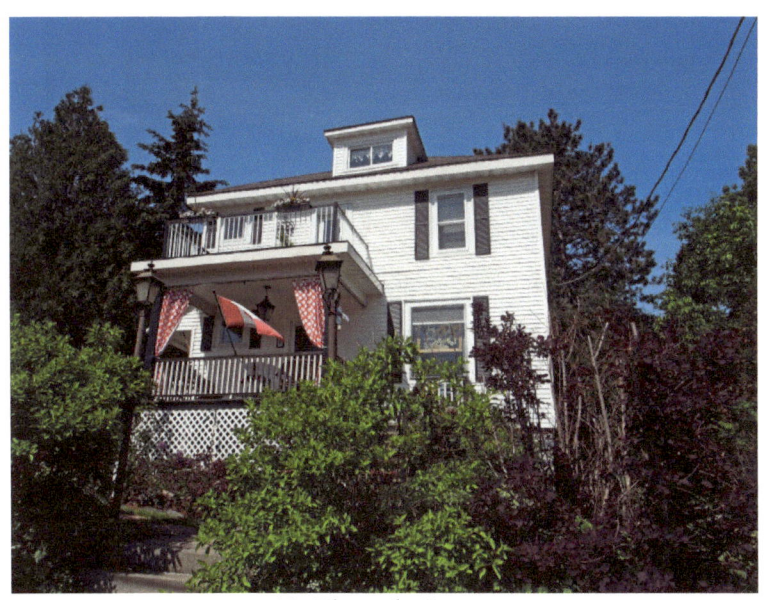

48 Church Street

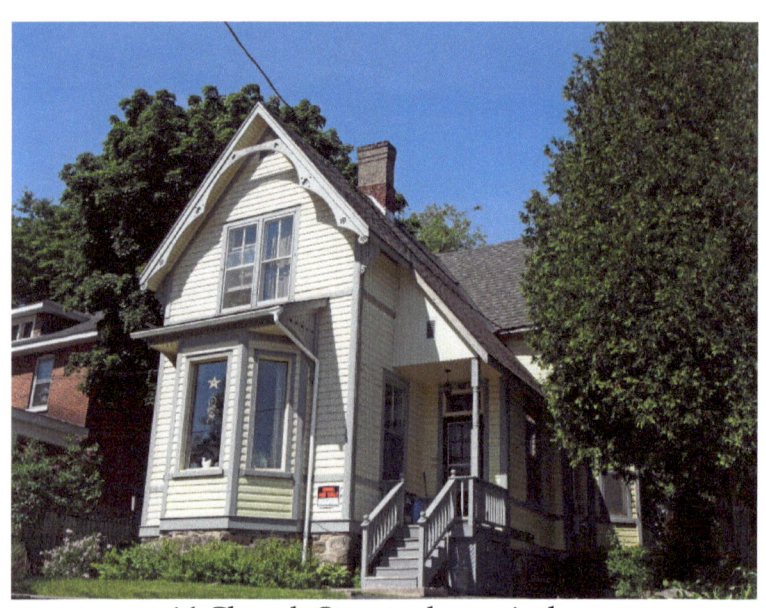
46 Church Street – bay window

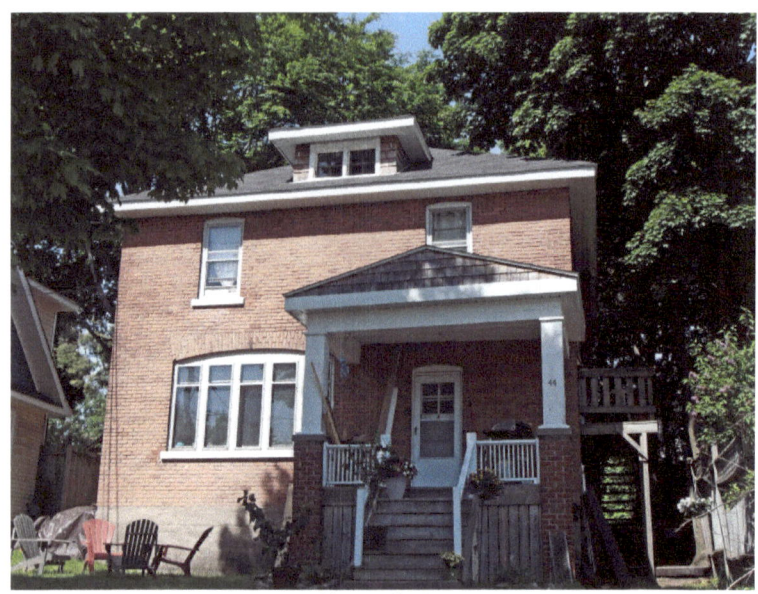
44 Church Street

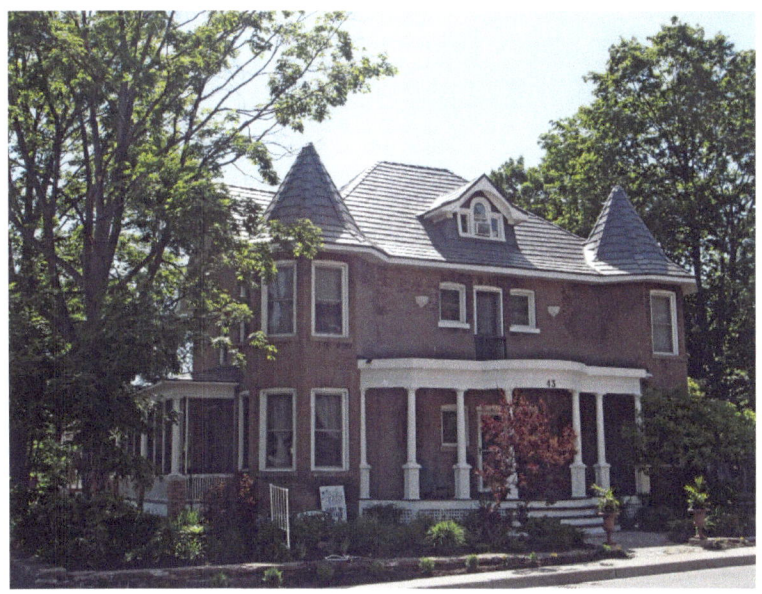

43 Church Street

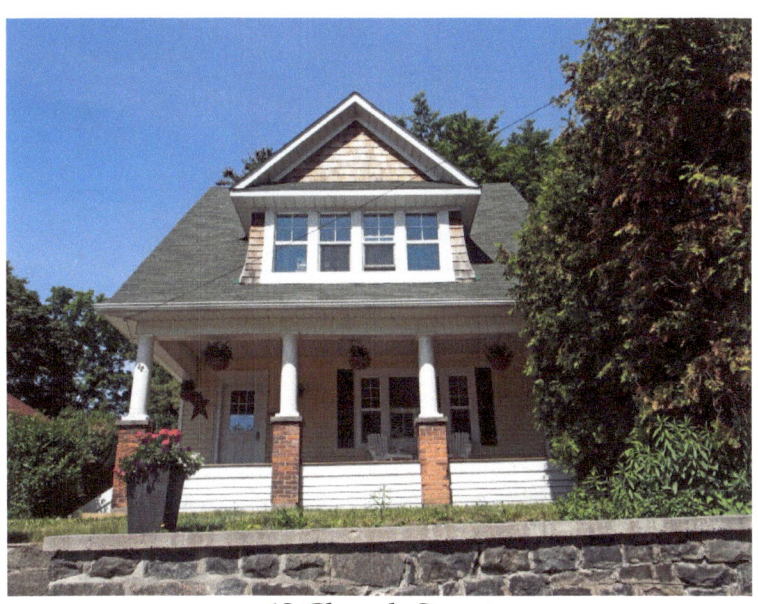

42 Church Street

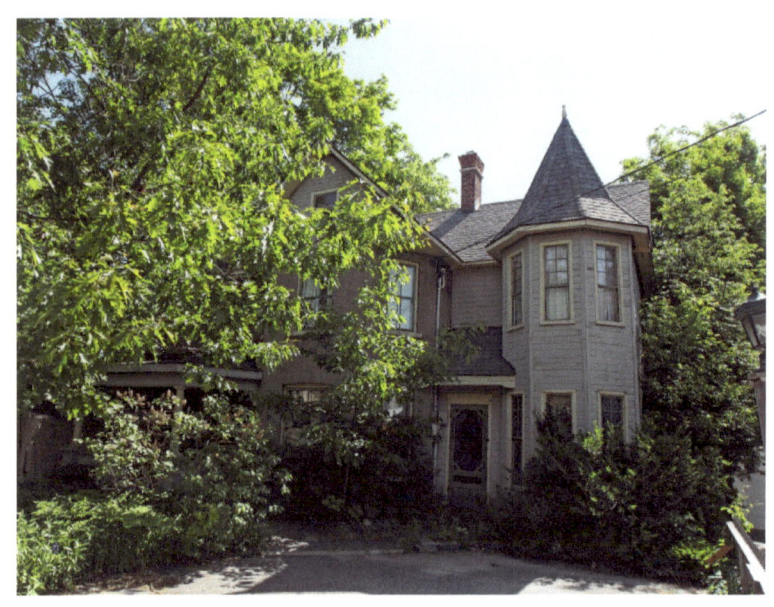

41 Church Street – two-story tower

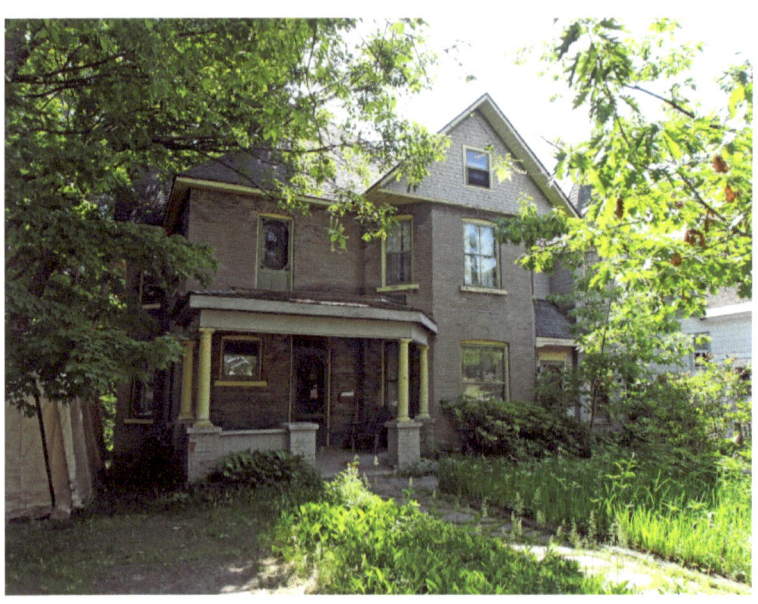

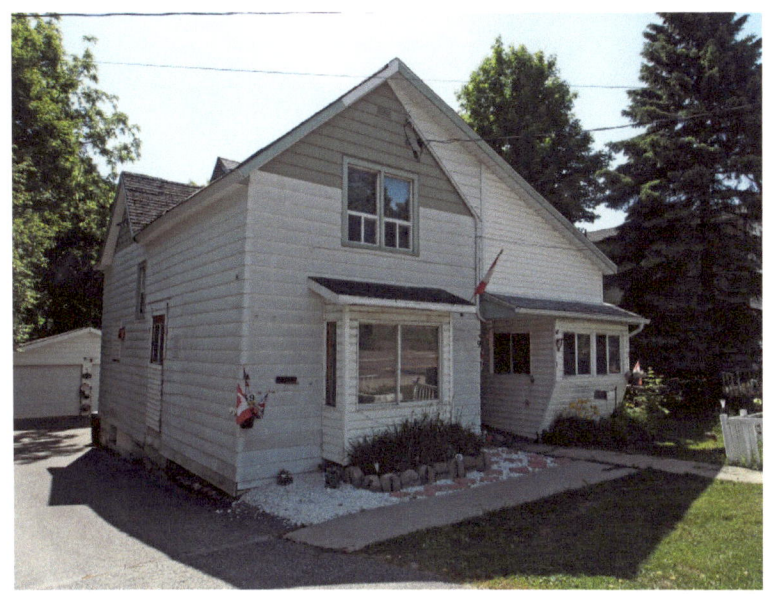

39 Church Street

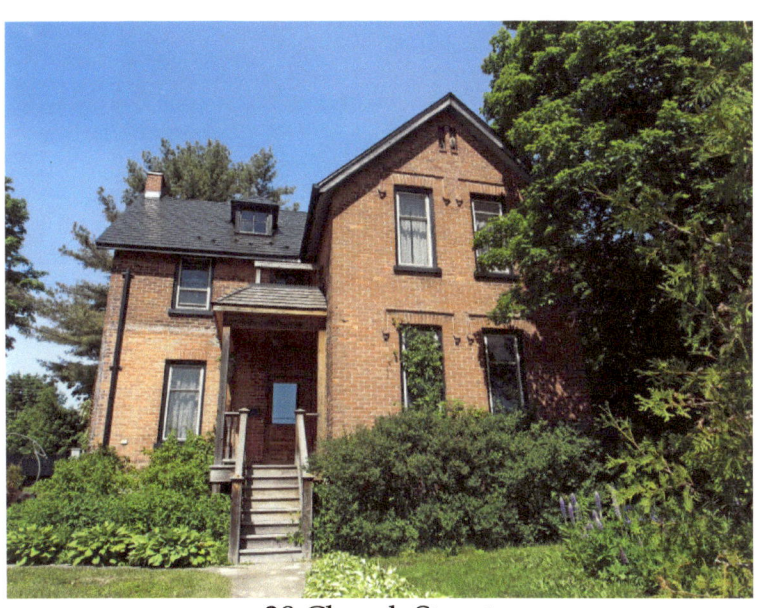

38 Church Street

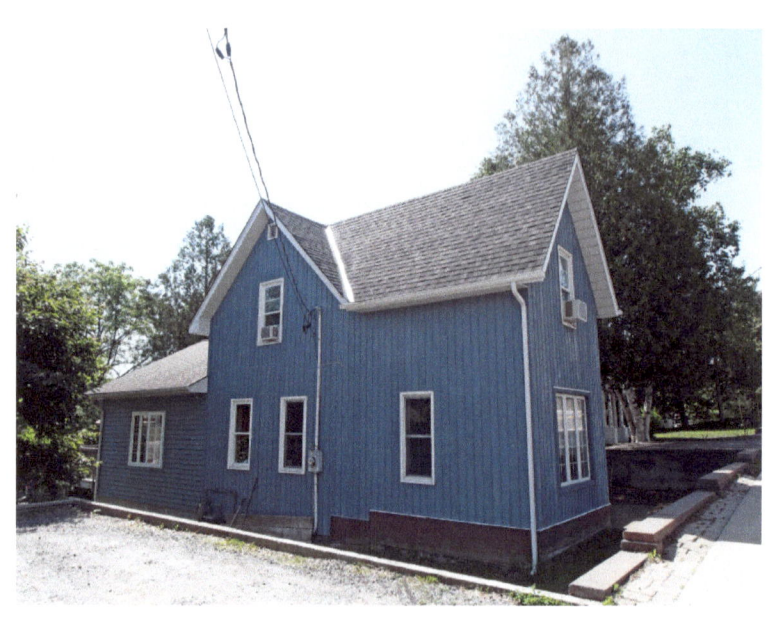

35 Church Street

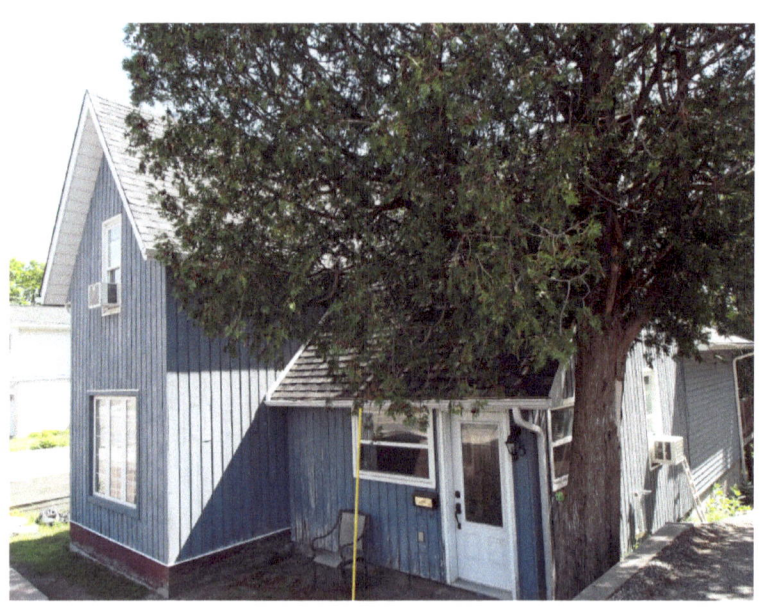

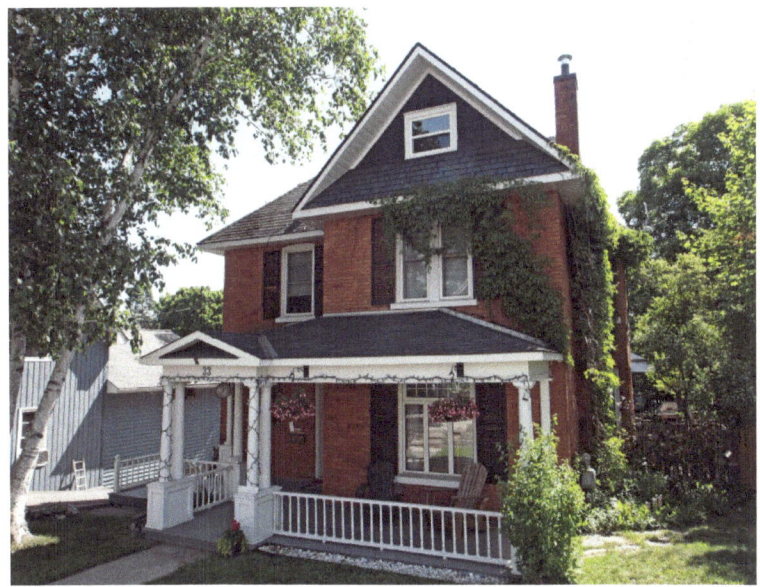

33 Church Street

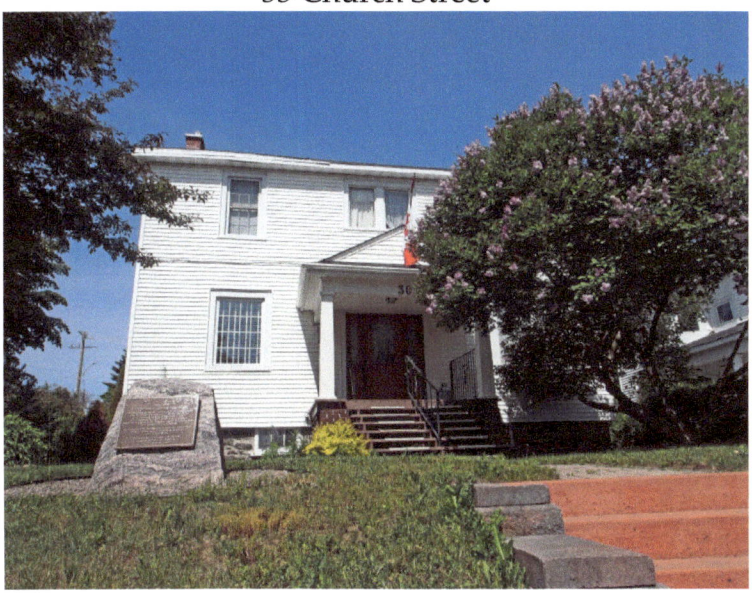

30 Church Street – The original plan of the town of Parry Sound shows this house as part of a five acre park known as Minnewawa Grove. William Beatty lived here with his bride Isabel Eliza Bowes; they raised five children.

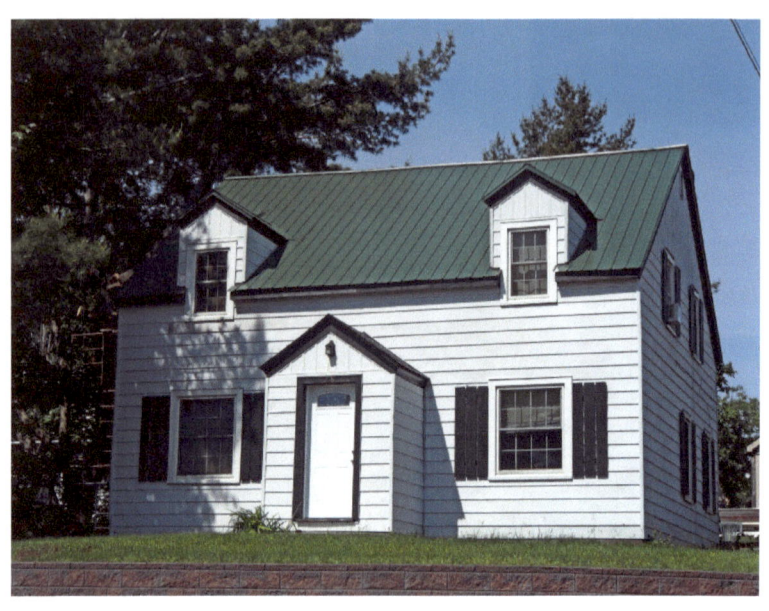

28 Church Street - dormers

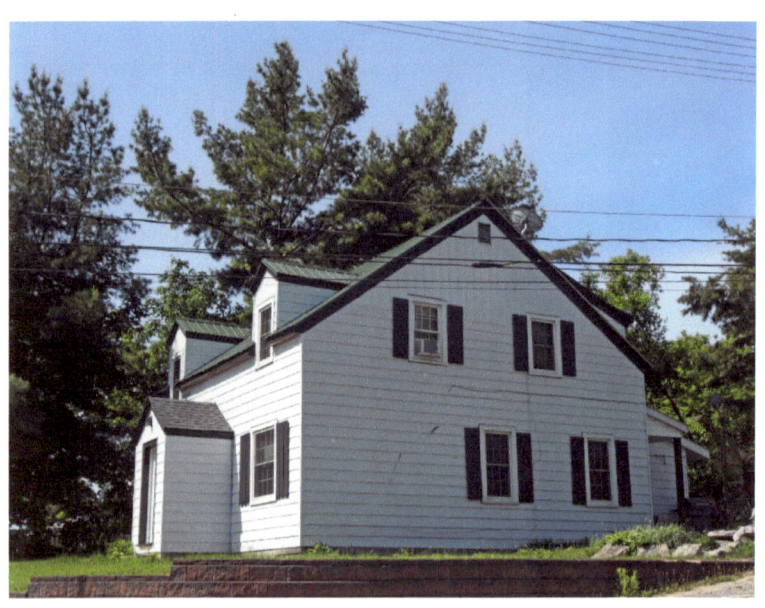

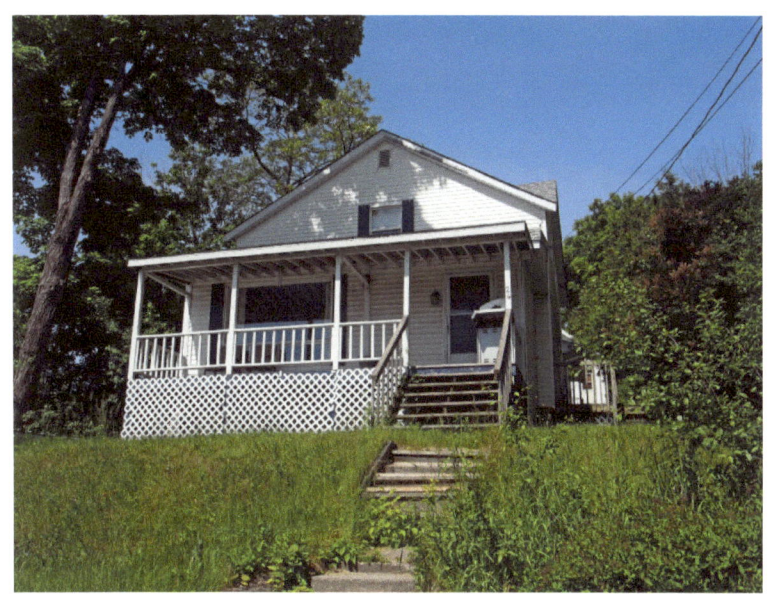

24 Church Street

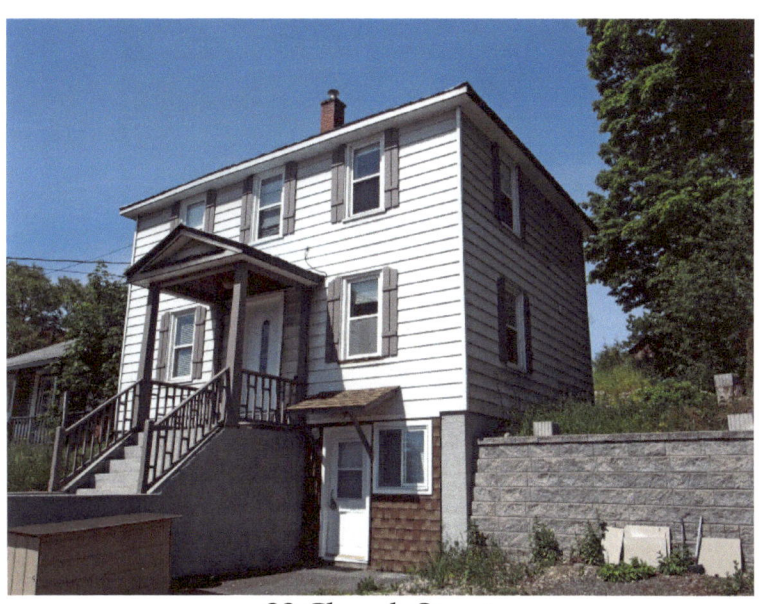

22 Church Street

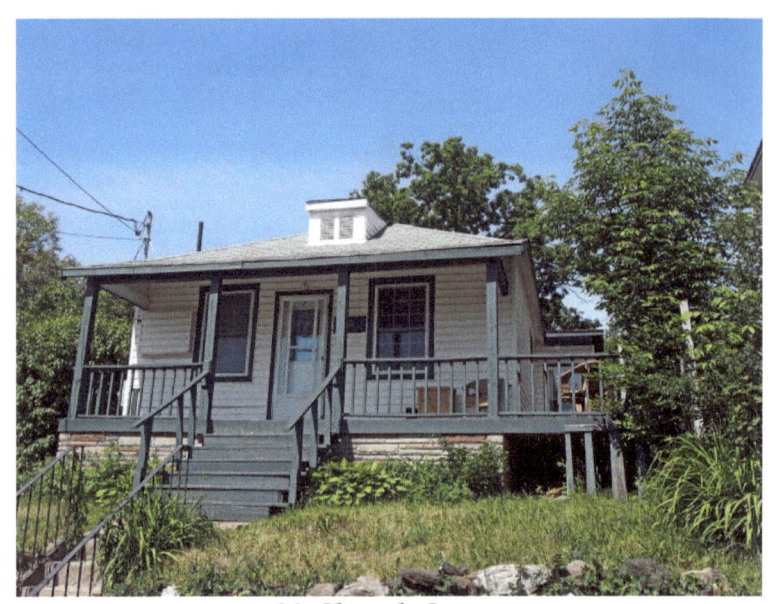

20 Church Street

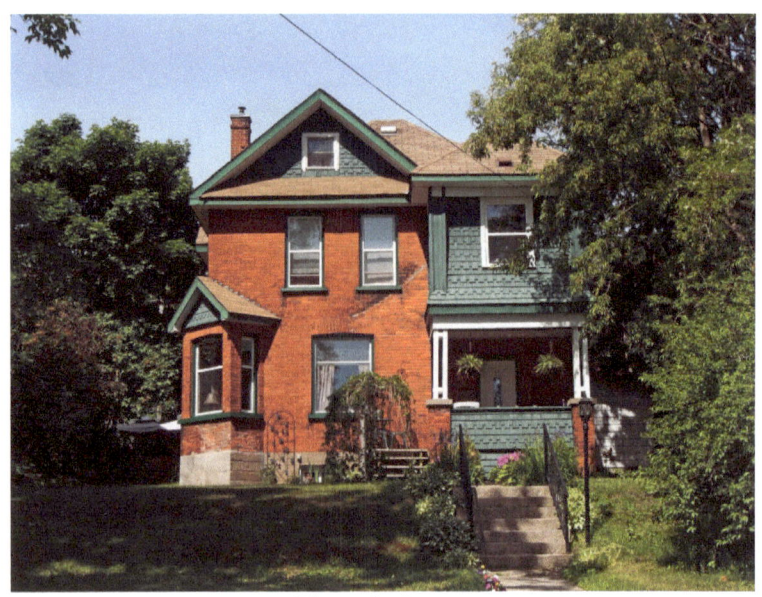

Church Street

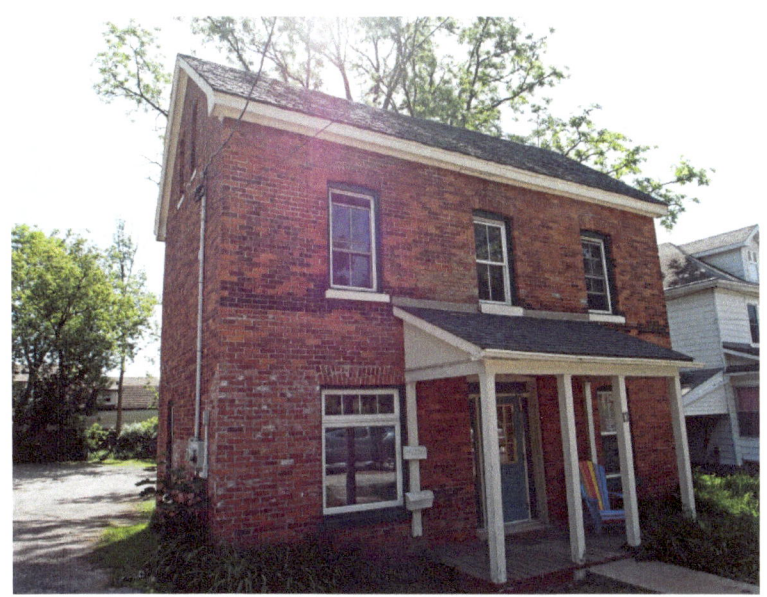

13 Church Street

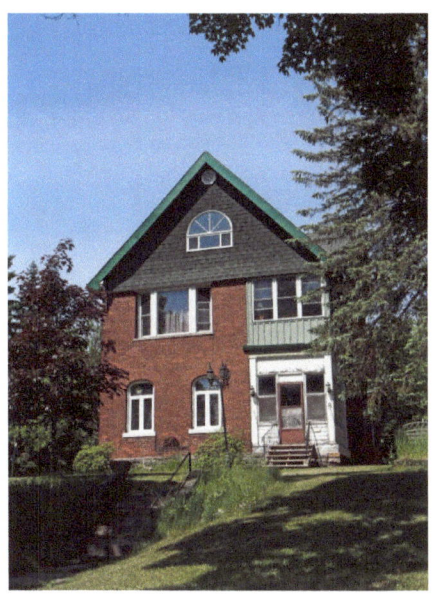

8 Church Street

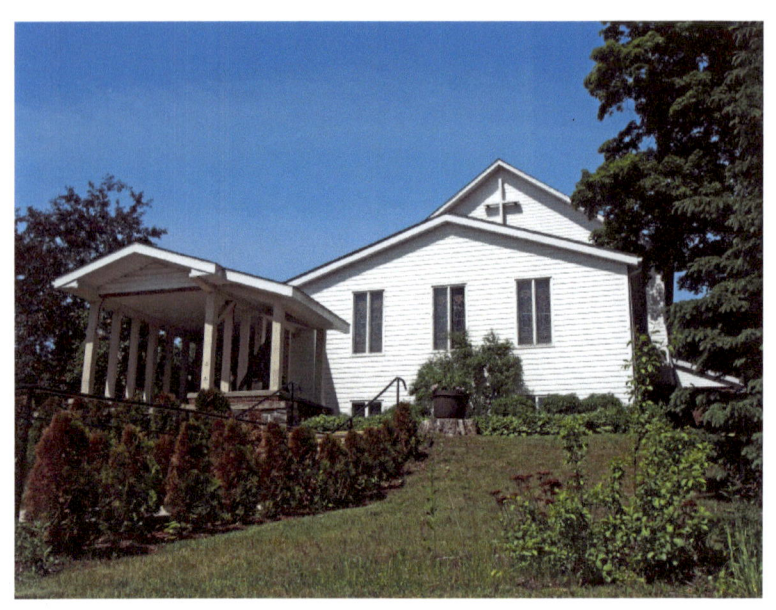

6 Church Street – Trinity Anglican Church

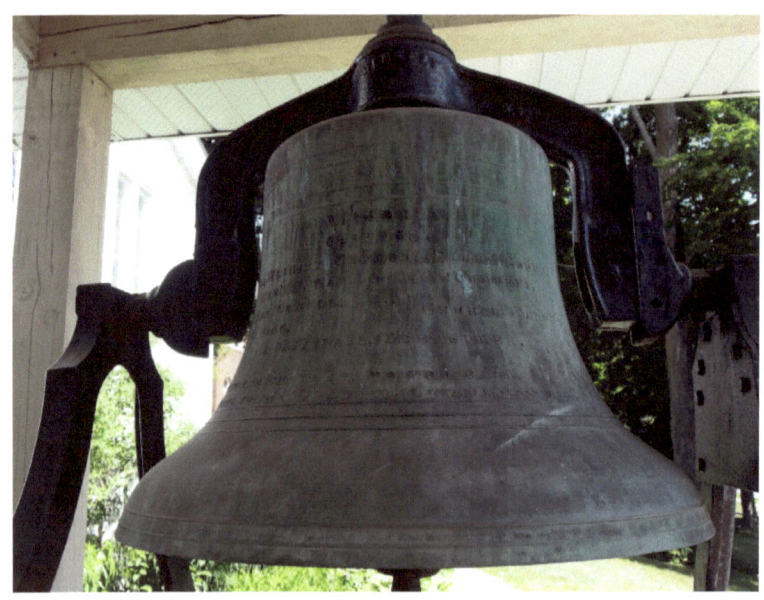

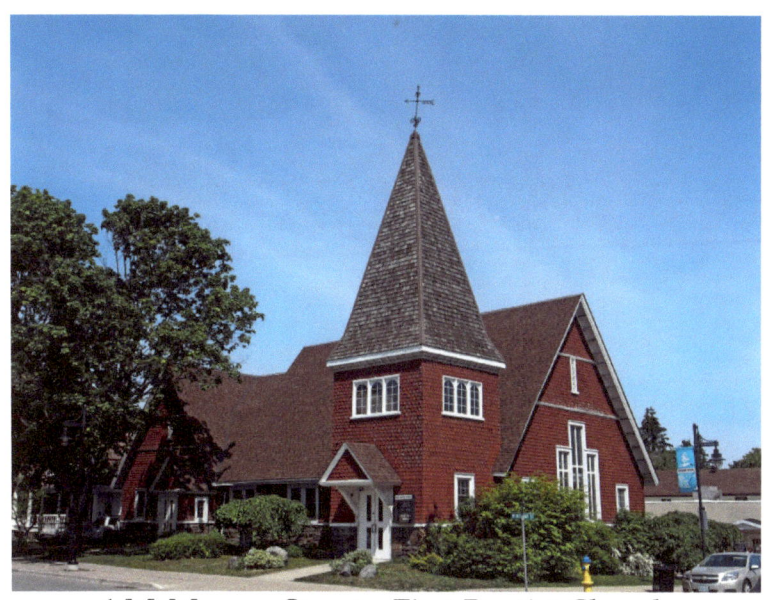

1 Mcmurray Street – First Baptist Church

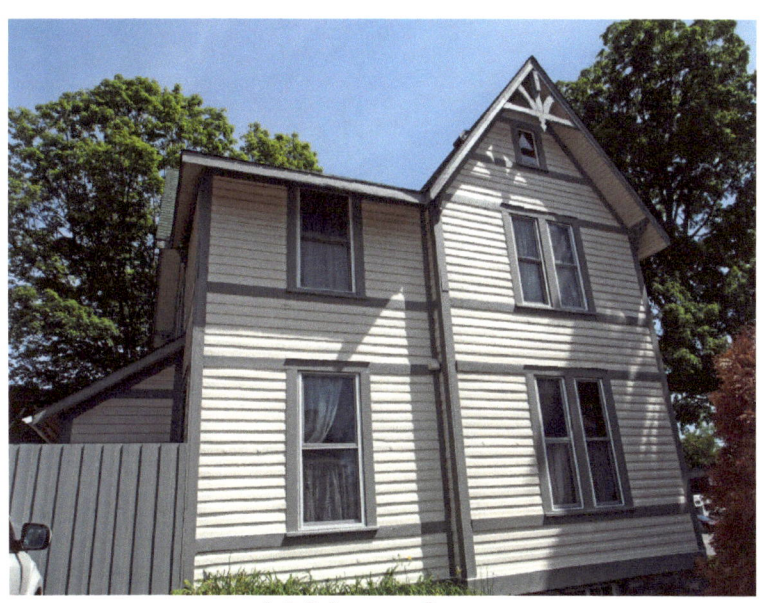

McMurray Street

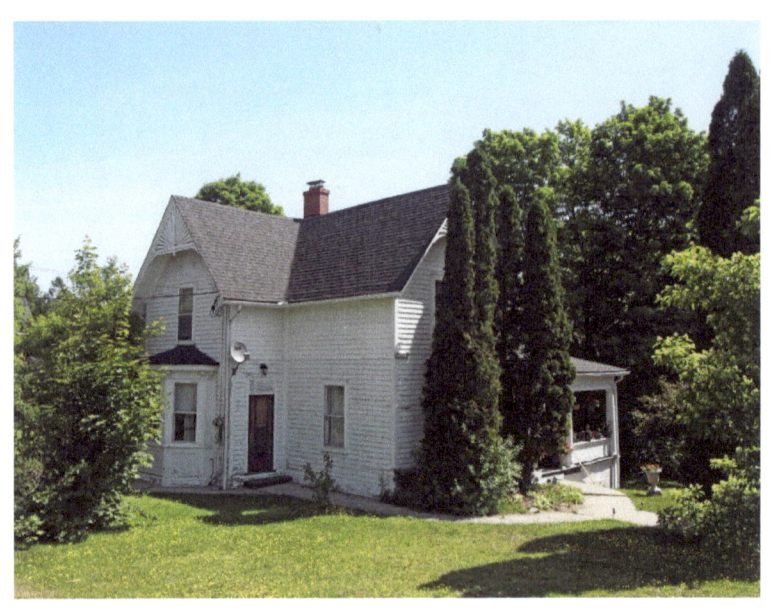

11 McMurray Street – sunburst detailing on gable

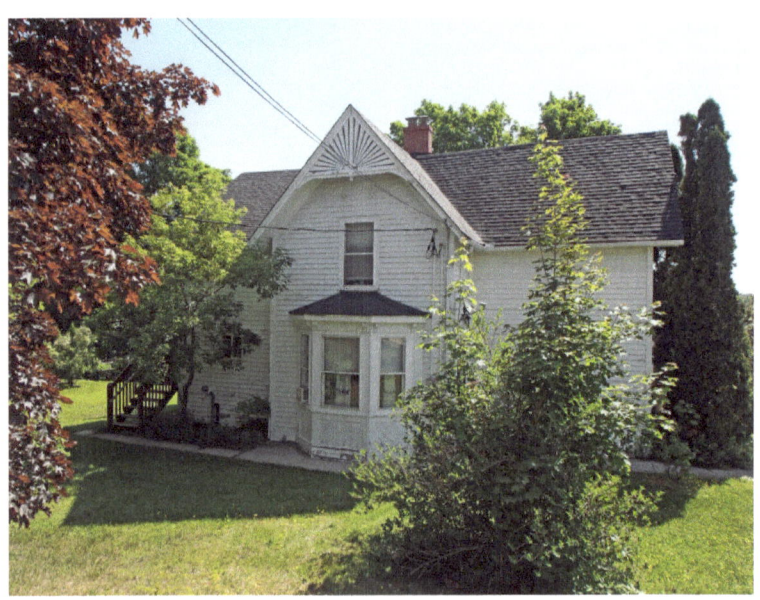

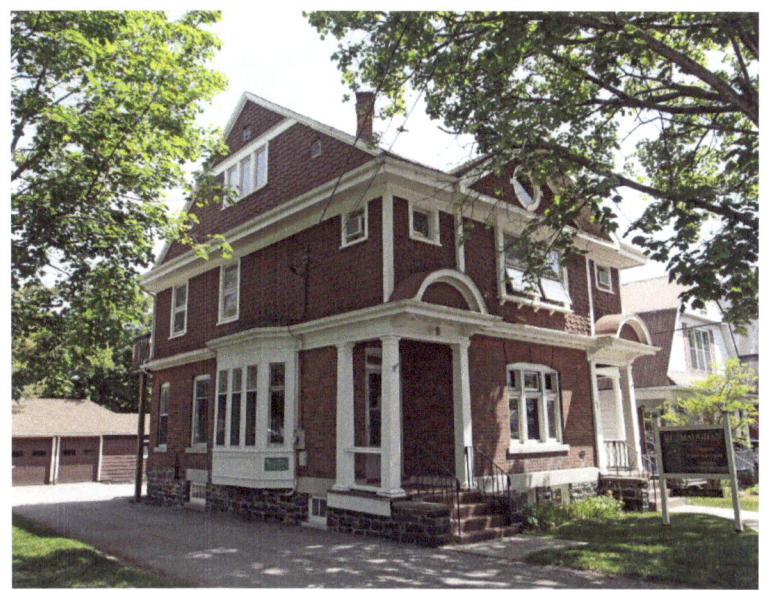

5 McMurray Street

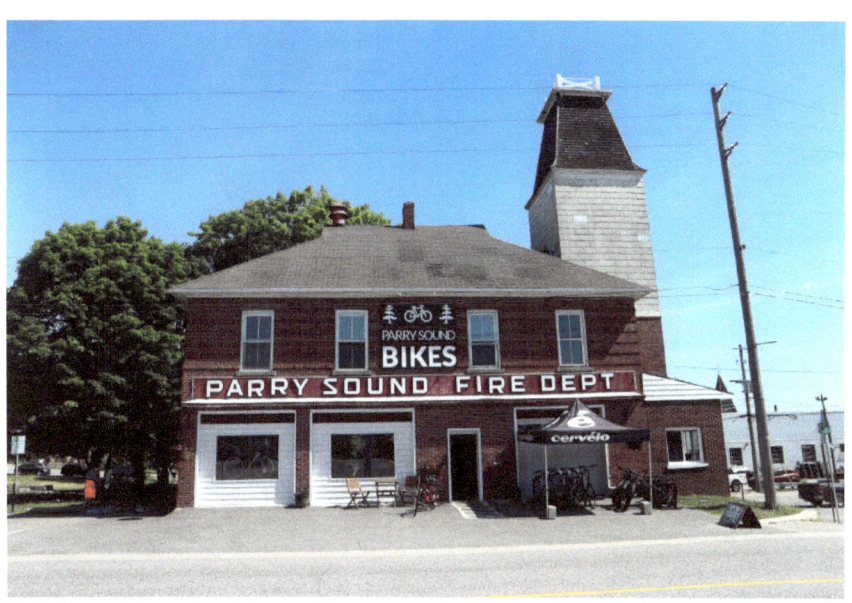

25 Mary Street – Parry Sound Bikes – Heritage Property - 1893

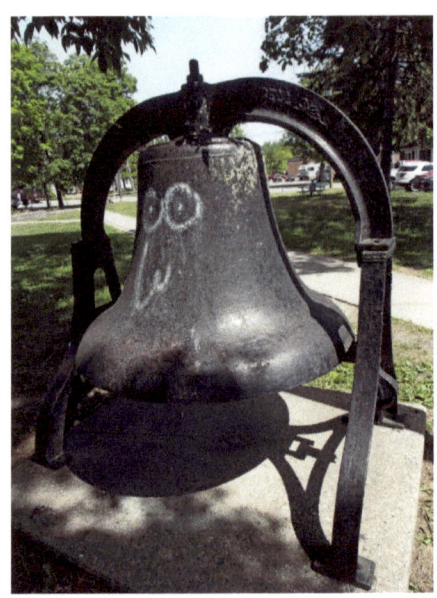

Bell in park

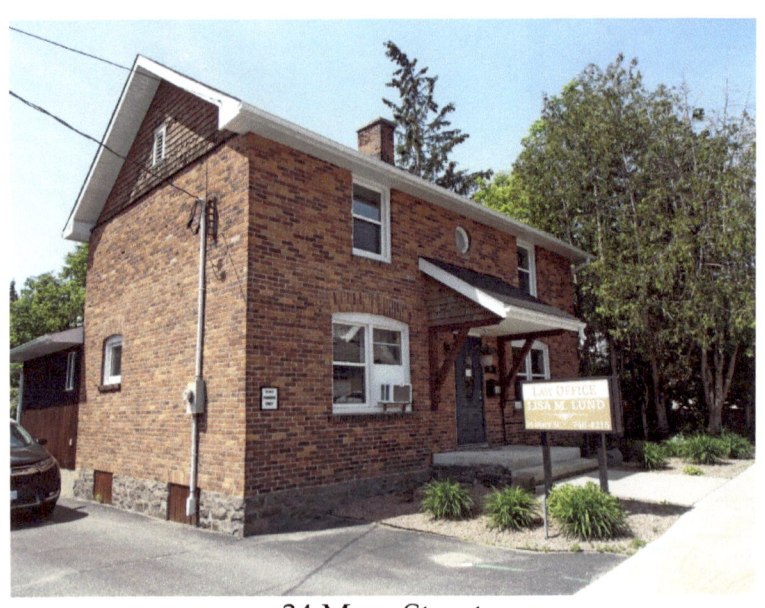

34 Mary Street

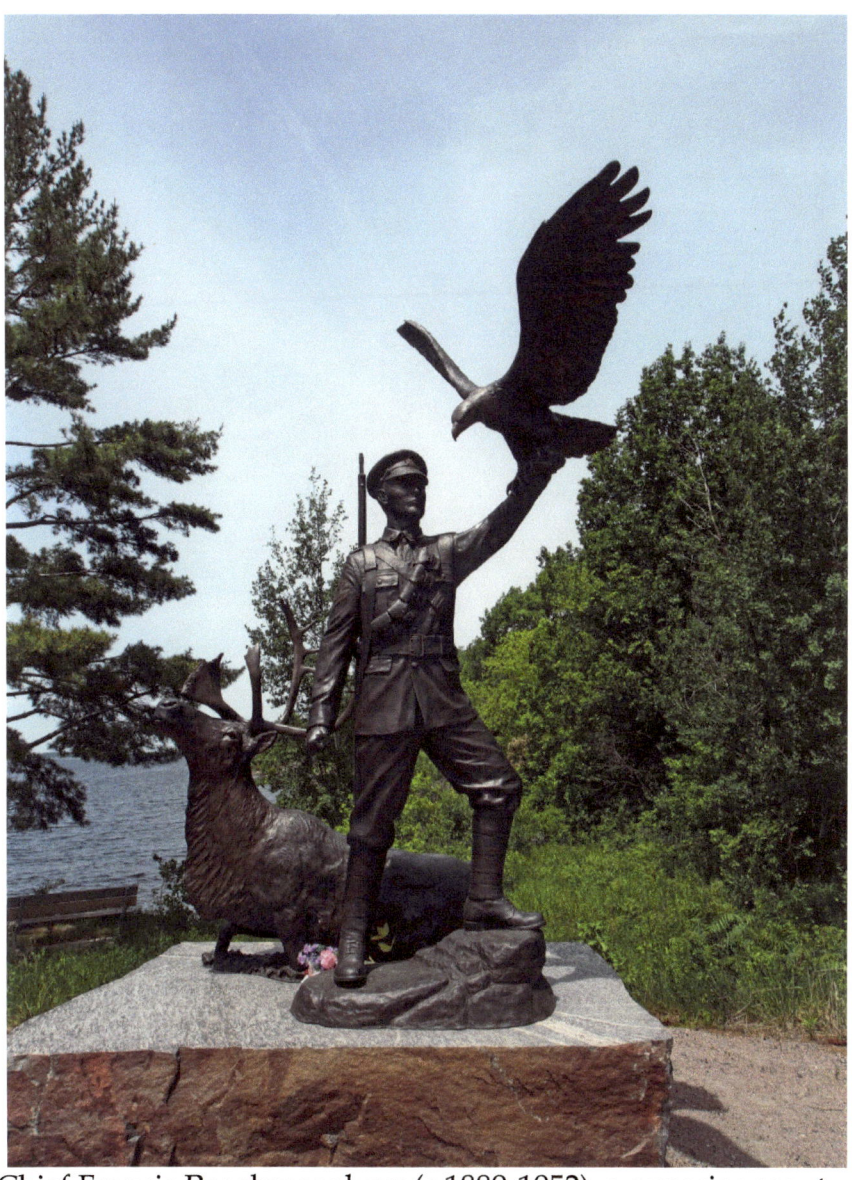

Chief Francis Pegahmagabow (c.1889-1952), a superior scout and sniper during World War I, served overseas with the Canadian Expeditionary Force. He received many battle awards. He was a passionate advocate for indigenous rights. Brave in war, brave in peace.

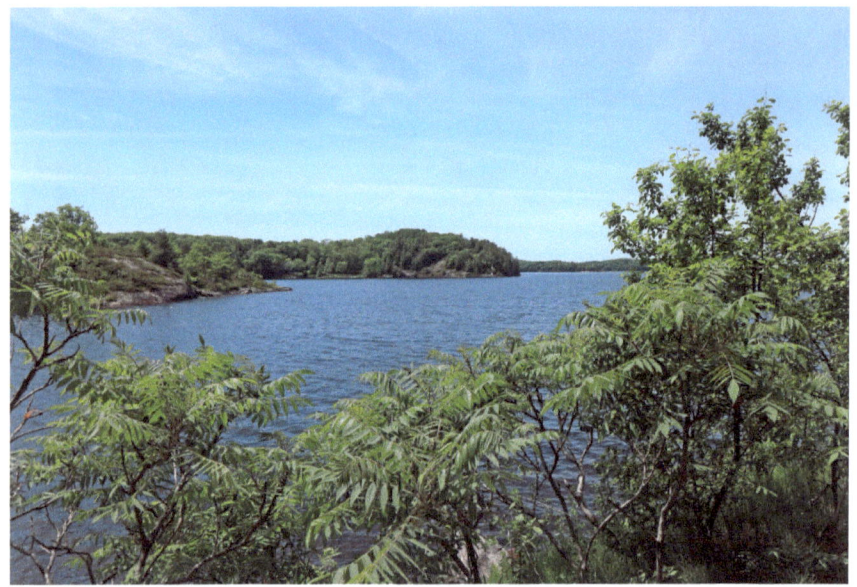

The Waterfront Trail follows the rocky shoreline along the Town of Parry Sound for six kilometers along a former railway line beside Georgian Bay.

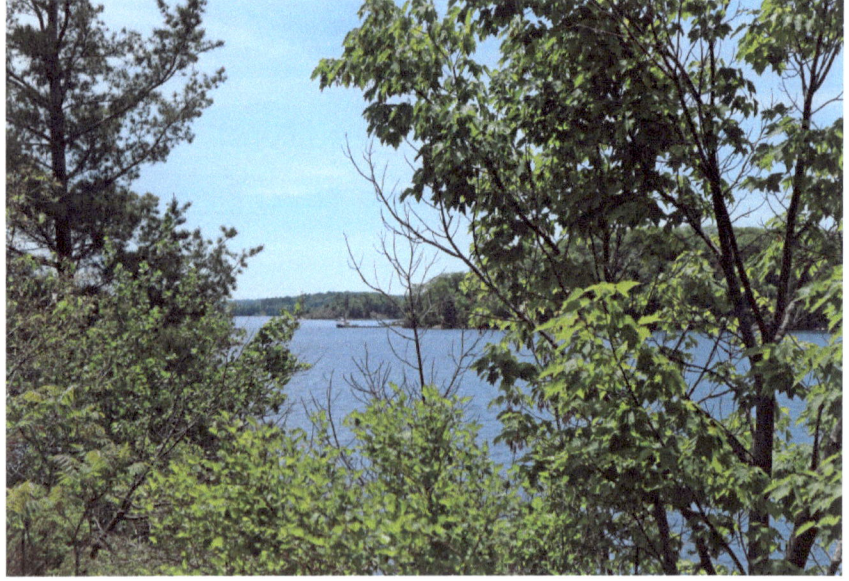

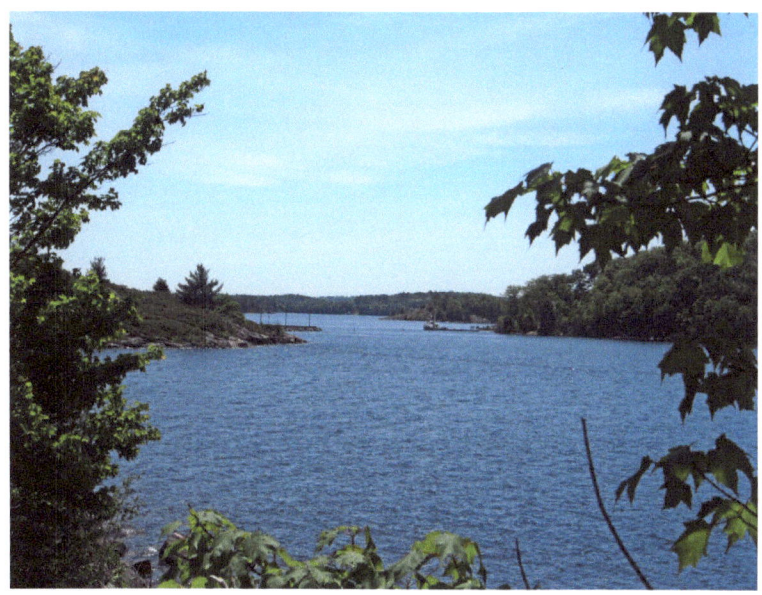

The Parry Sound coastline is home to the Georgian Bay Biosphere Reserve, one of thirteen UNESCO sites in Canada.

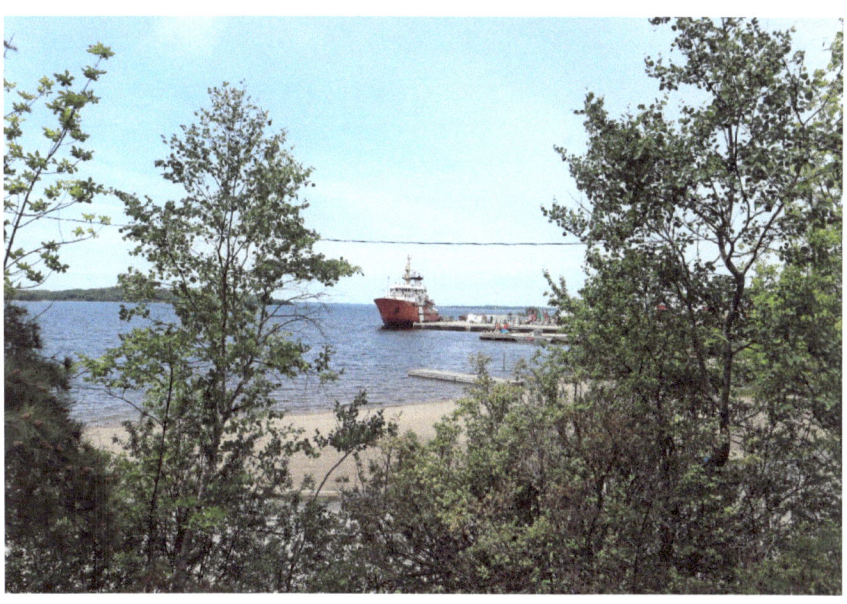

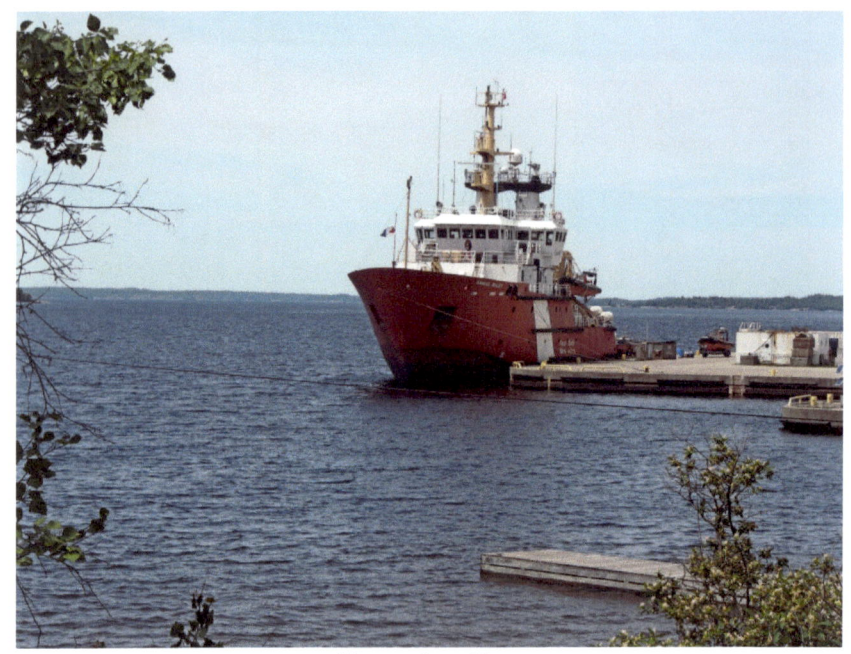
Georgian Bay

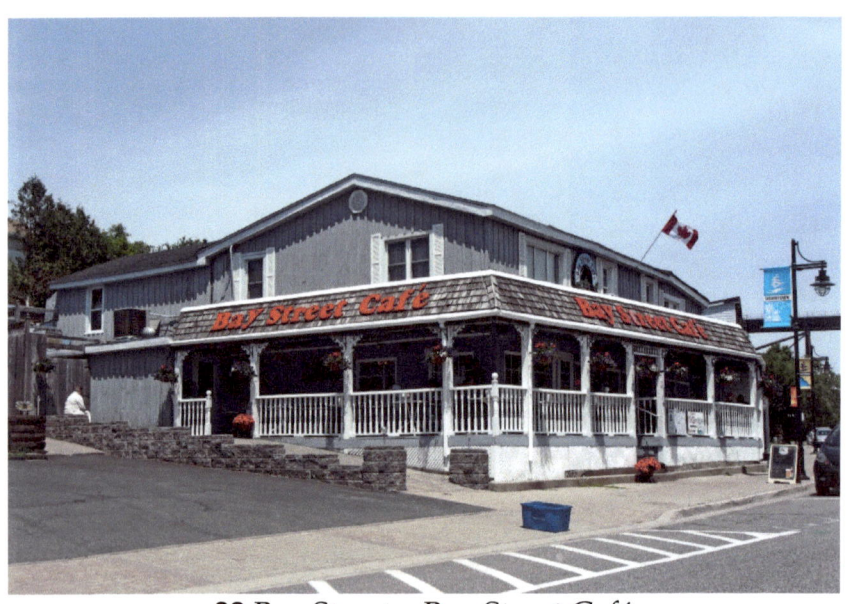
22 Bay Street – Bay Street Café

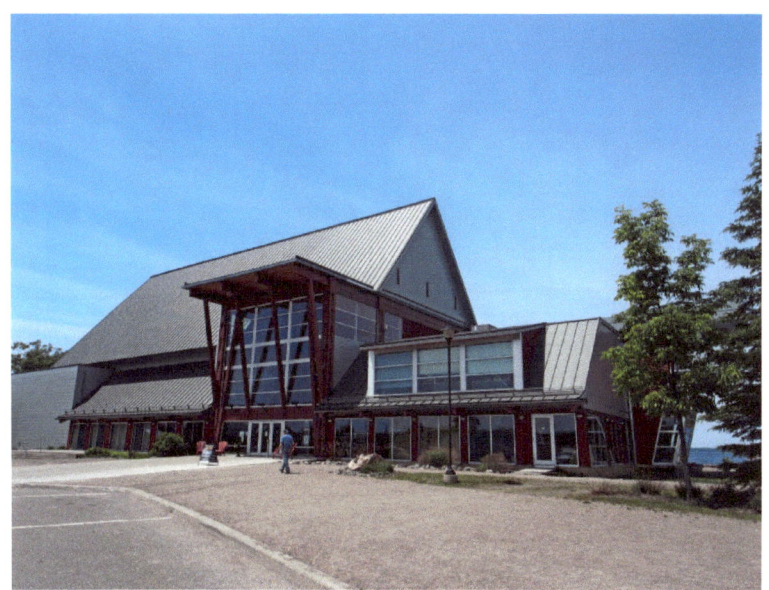

2 Bay Street - Charles W. Stockey Centre for the Performing Arts overlooks Georgian Bay and has a 415 seat acoustically perfect performance hall. The Bobby Orr Hall of Fame is an interactive sports heritage museum paying tribute to hometown hockey legend, Bobby Orr, and other exceptional athletes with connections to Parry Sound.

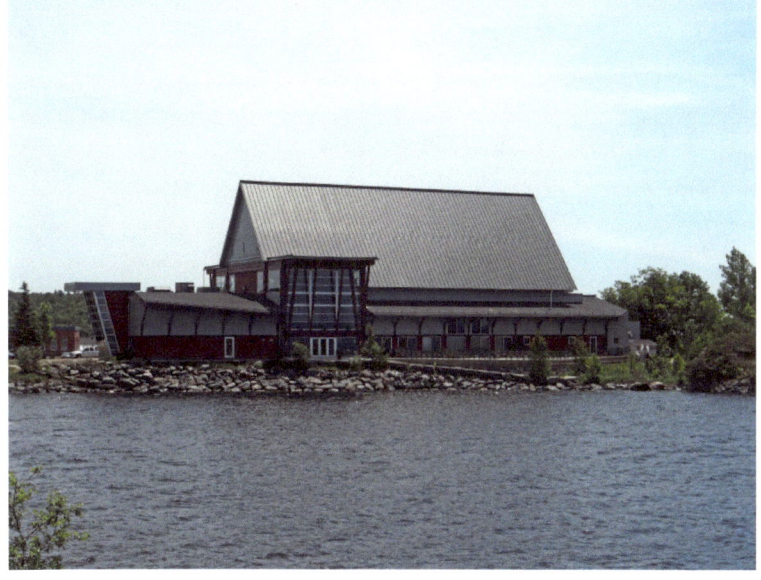

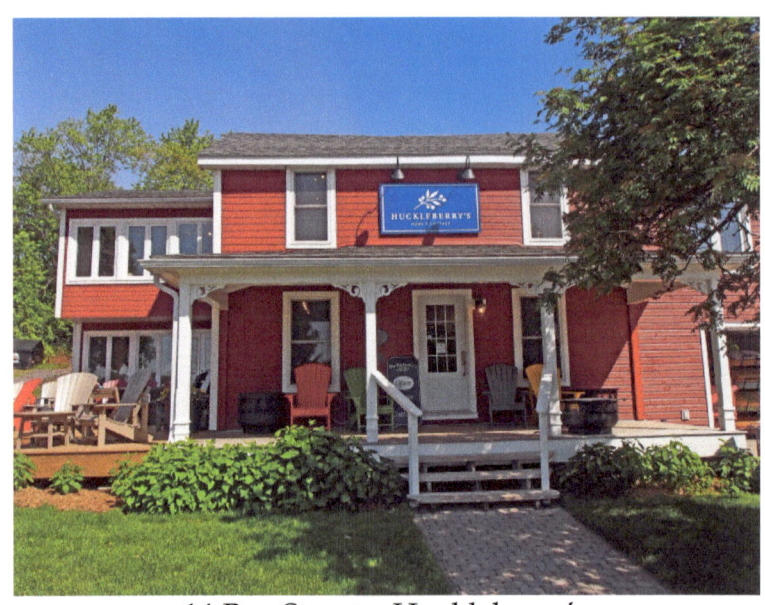

14 Bay Street – Huckleberry's

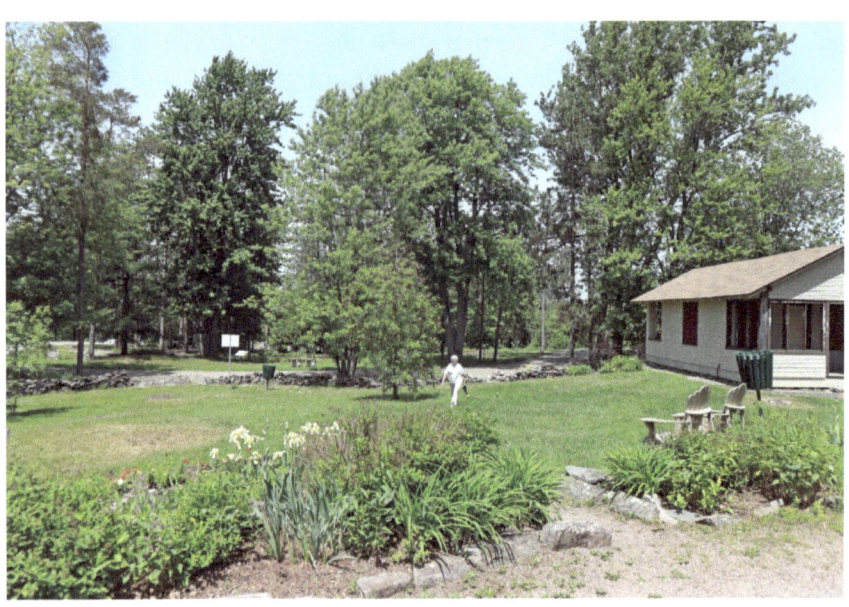

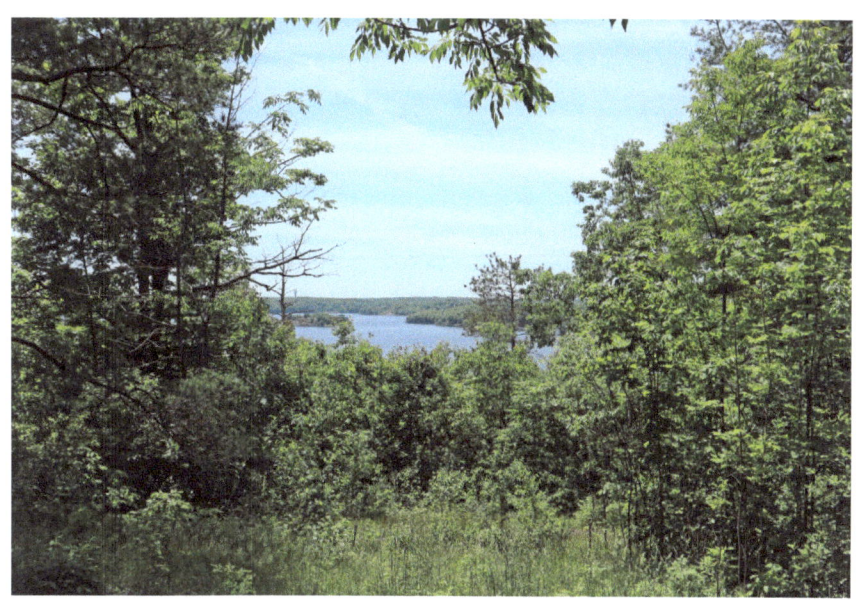

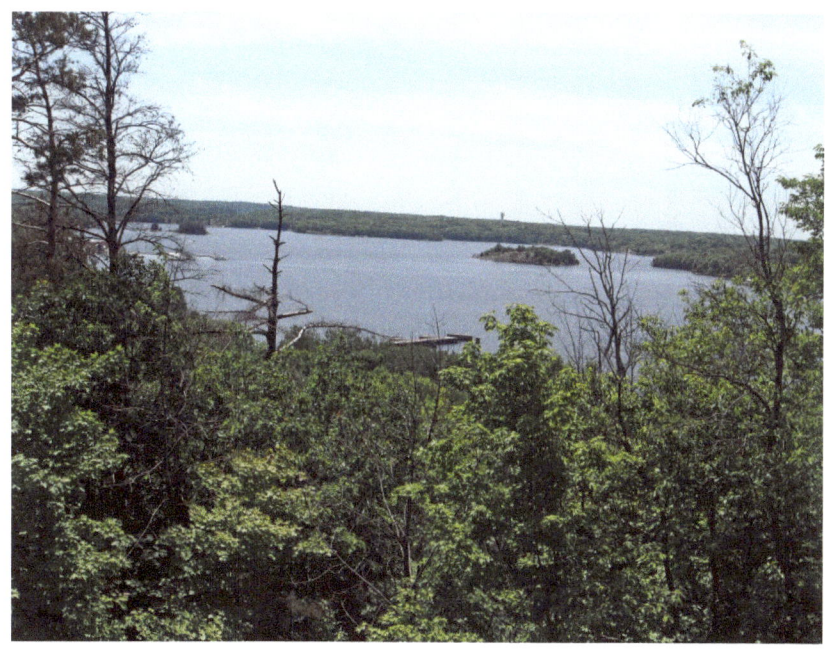

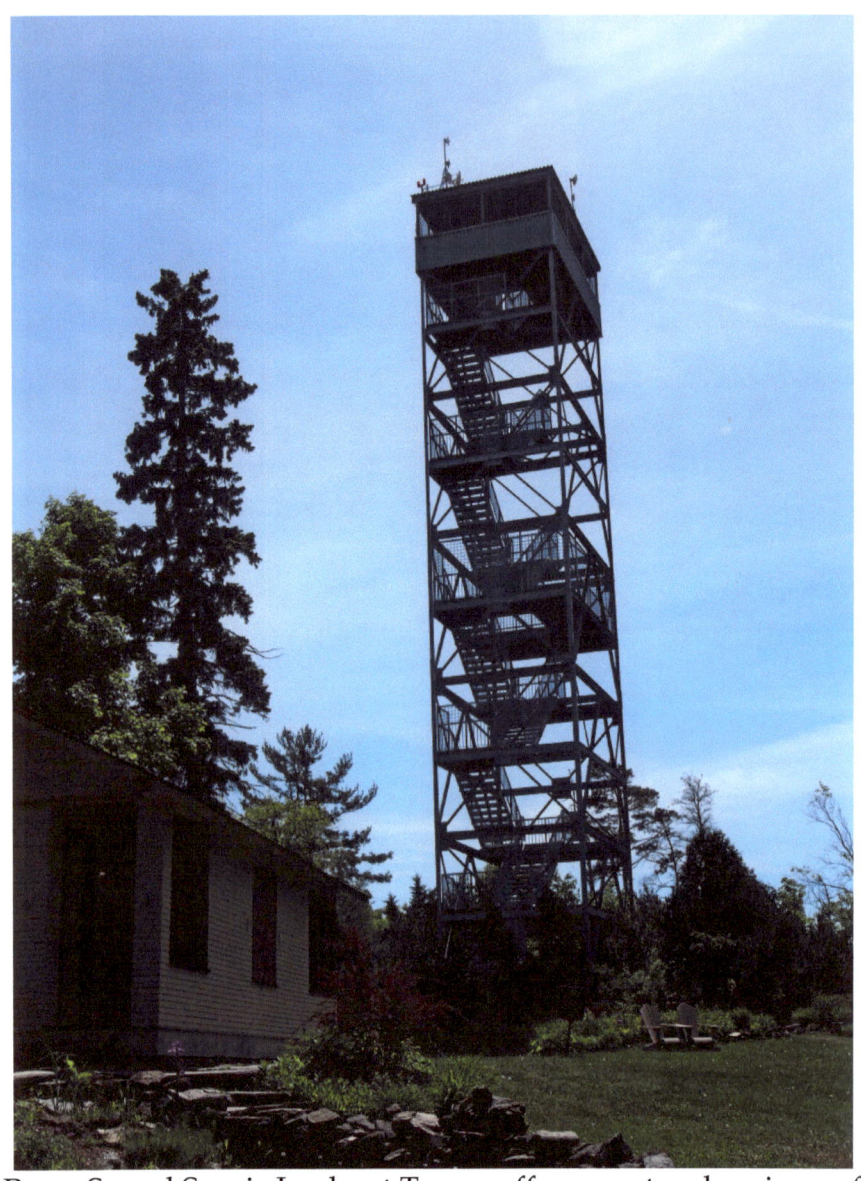

Parry Sound Scenic Lookout Tower offers spectacular views of the harbor and Georgian Bay. Climb 30 meters up a historic fire observation tower to enjoy a spectacular 360 view of Parry Sound.

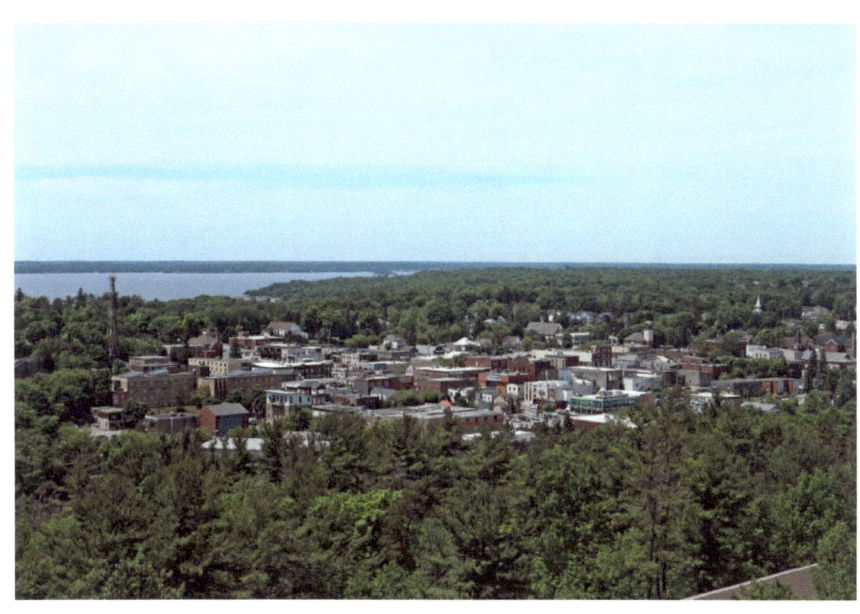

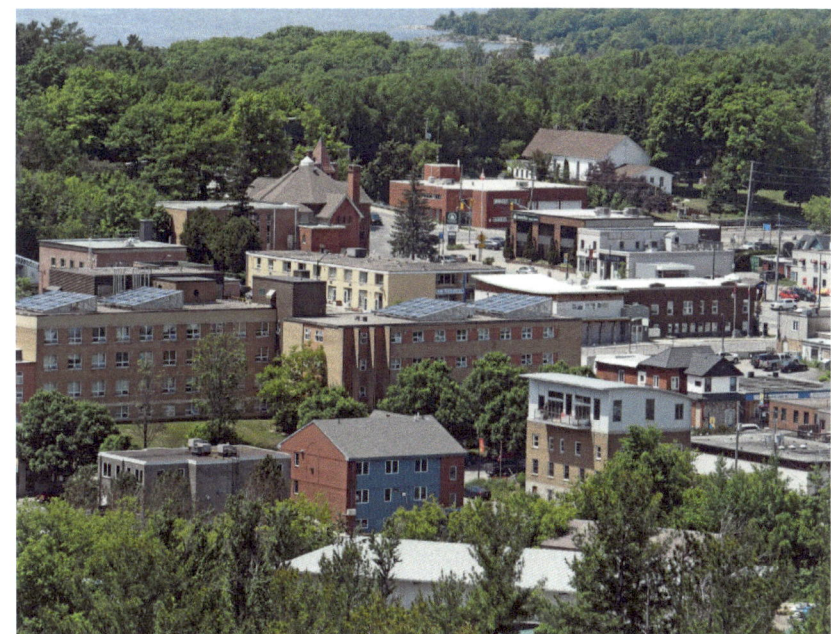

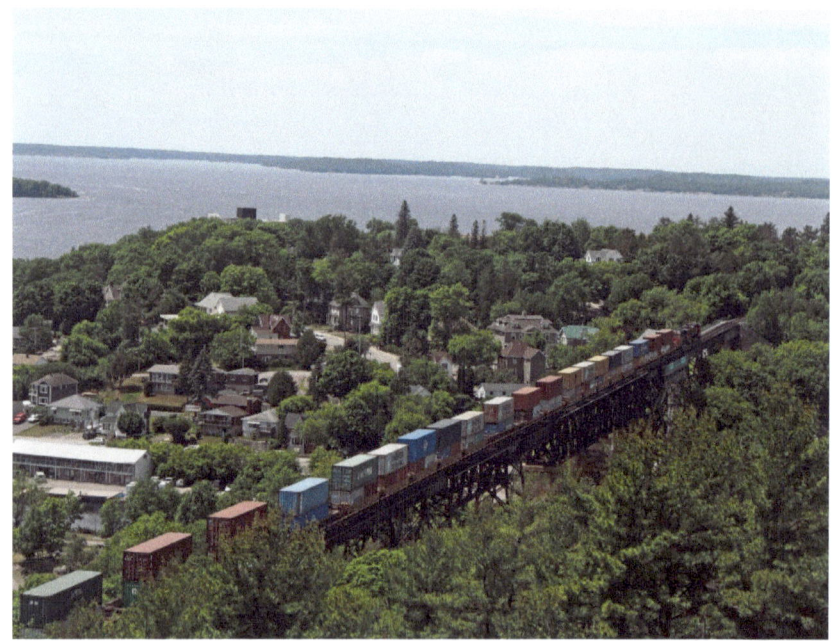

CPR Train Trestle — Spanning the Seguin River, at 105 feet high and about 1700 feet in length the old train bridge is a local icon.

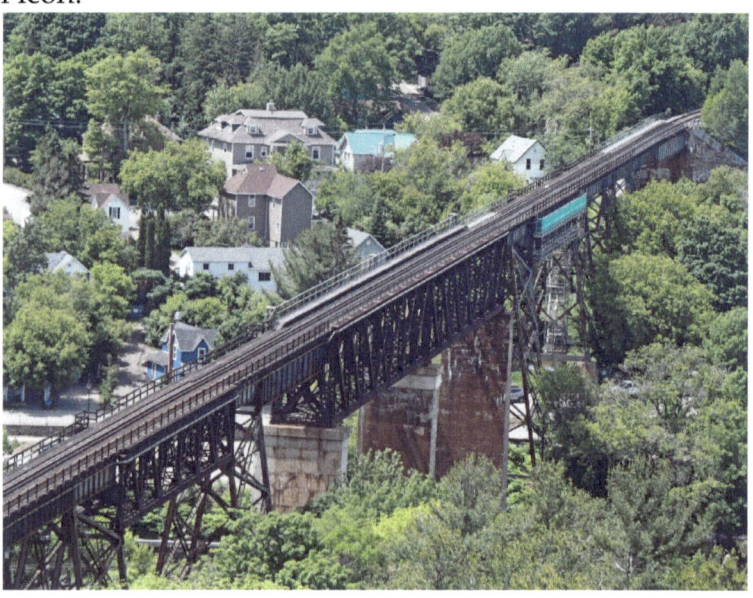

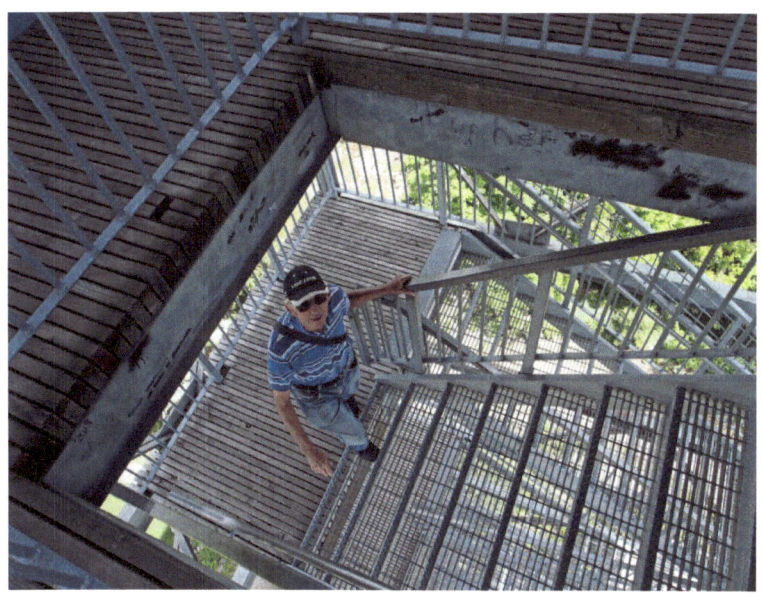

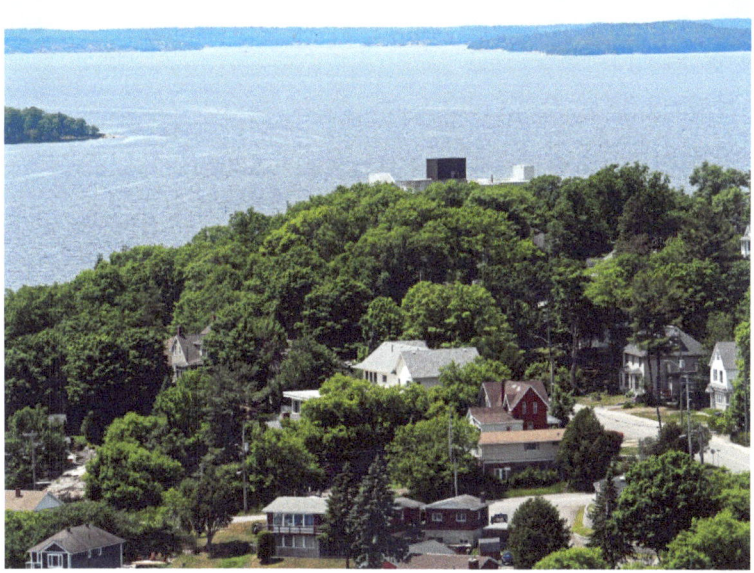

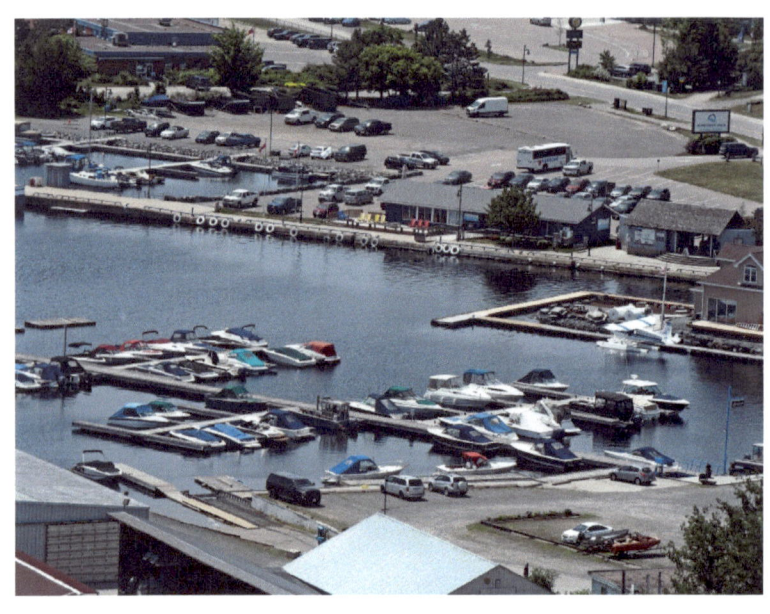

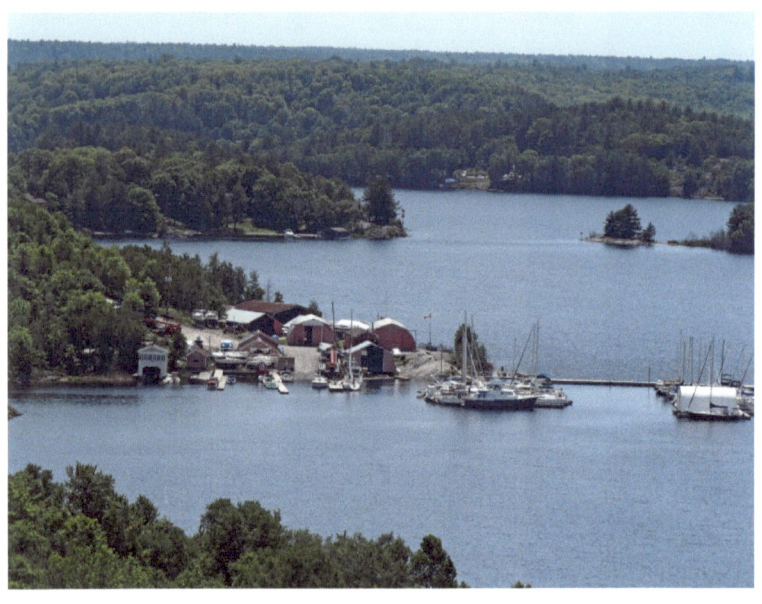

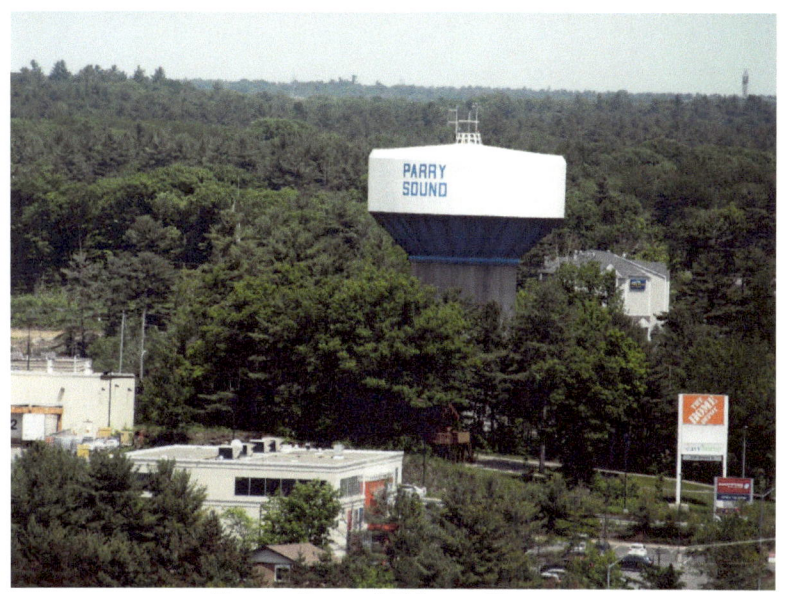

Parry Sound Water Tower

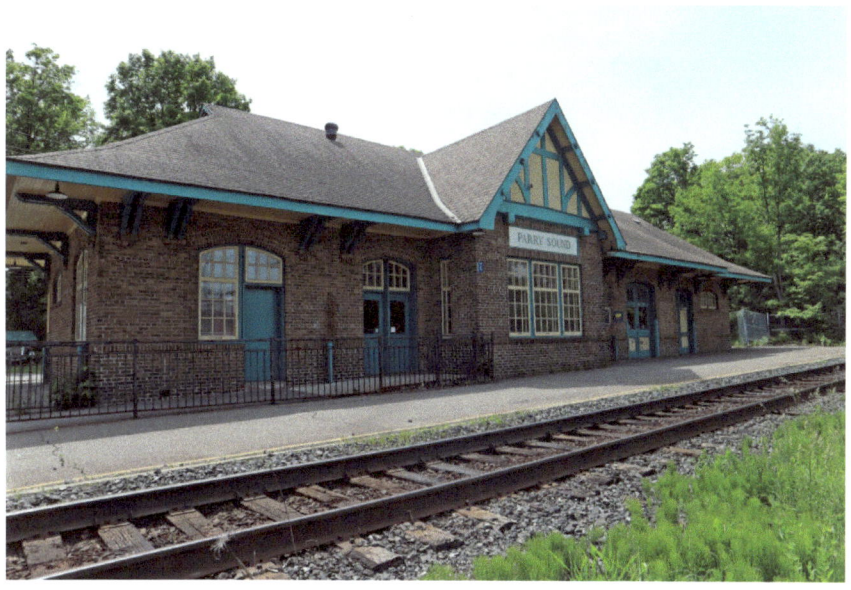

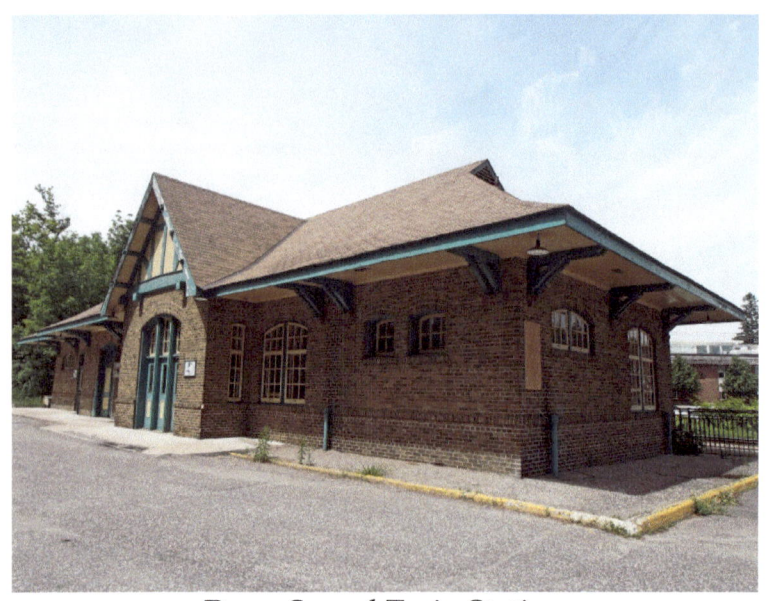

Parry Sound Train Station

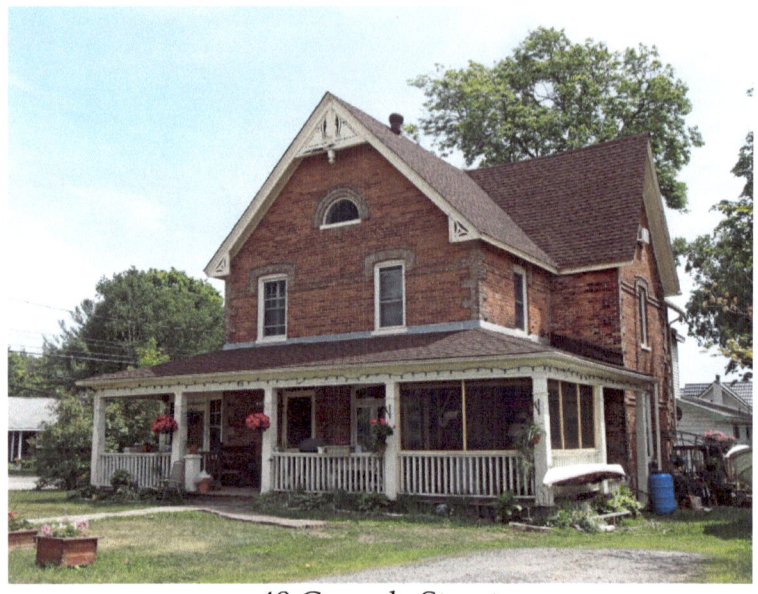

48 Cascade Street

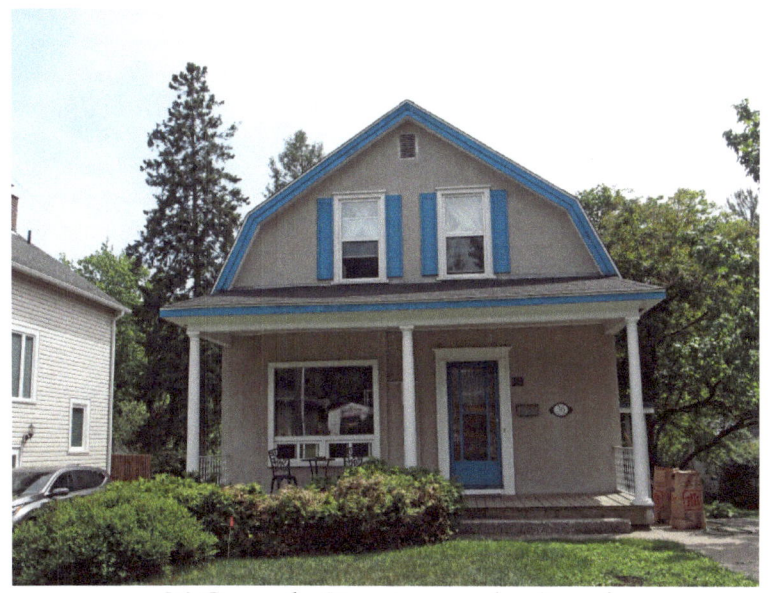

36 Cascade Street – gambrel roof

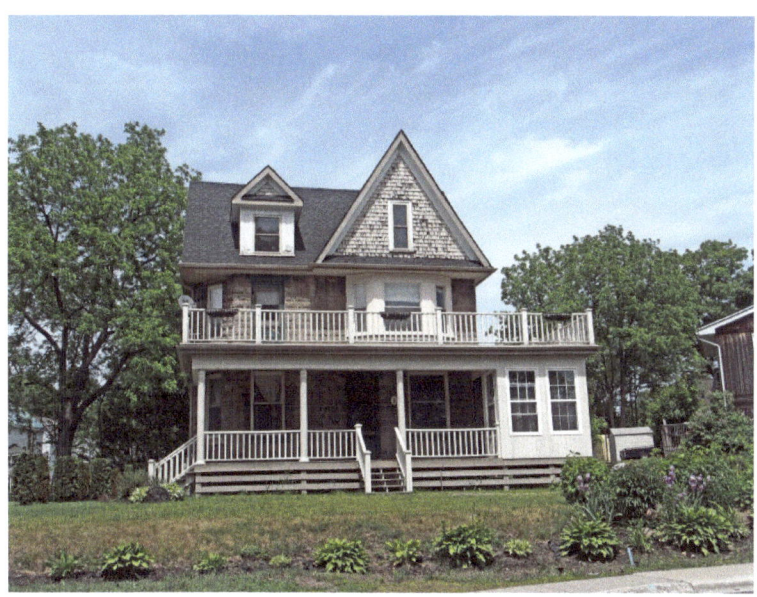

Cascade Street

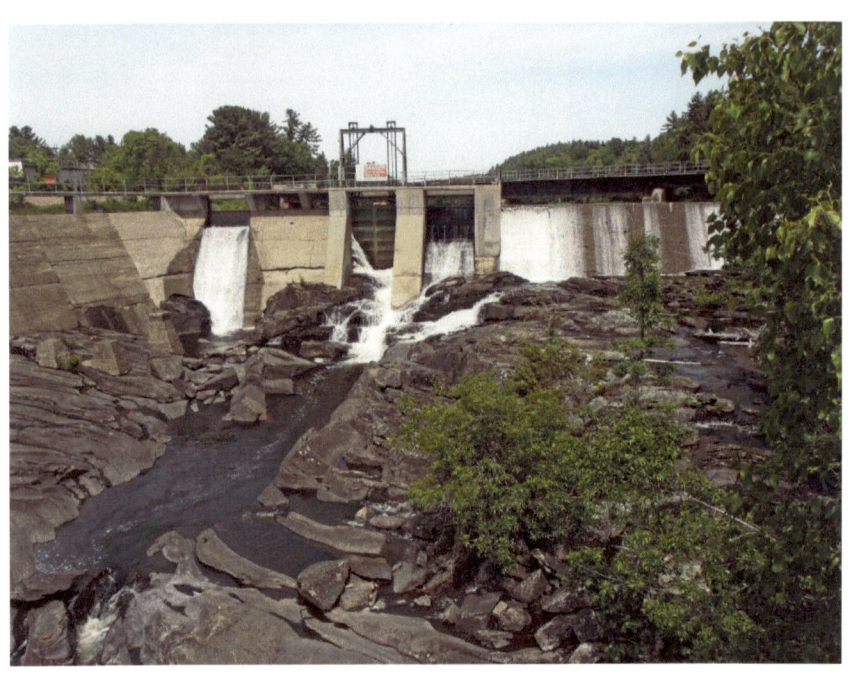

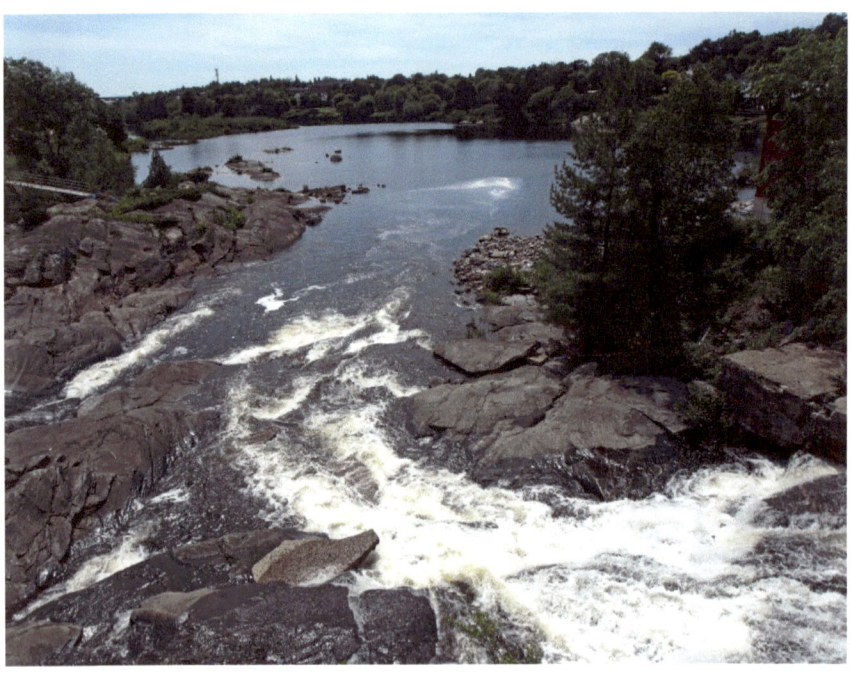

Other Books by Barbara Raue

Coins of Gold
Arrows, Indians and Love
The Life and Times of Barbara
The Cromwell Family Book
Laura Secord Discovered
Daddy Where Are You?

Montana Series
Book 1: Montana Dream
Book 2: Life on the Montana Frontier
Book 3: Montana to Boston and Back
Book 4: Montana Sons Go to War
Book 5: Montana Sons Return from War

Donaldson Series
Book 1: Rite of Passage
Book 2: Rite of Marriage

© 2022 by Barbara Raue - All the photos in this book have been taken with my cameras. I own the rights to them.

Barbara is The Authority on Saving Our History One Photo at a Time. She is pursuing her interest in photography and architecture by preserving a record through photos of old buildings from the 1800s and 1900s with their unique architecture. Enjoy the beautiful architecture in the comfort of your living room. Dream about what it was like in those by-gone days. Dream about what it was like to live in a mansion like one of those in this book.

Barbara Raue, a wife, mother and grandmother, is an avid reader and writer. She has researched and compiled several family histories. In 2010, Barbara published her book "Coins of Gold," which celebrates the courageous life of her mother, May Todd. Barbara's second book is a historical fiction "Arrows, Indians and Love" which takes place in Boonesborough, Kentucky during the time of Daniel Boone. In 2013, Barbara published *The Cromwell Family Book* in which she traces her ancestry generations back into Great Britain. Her second novel is called *Laura Secord Discovered,* in which the story of Laura's service during the War of 1812 is shared. Barbara's memoir is titled *Daddy Where Are You?* It tells of her life growing up without a father. Five novels in the Montana Series have been published, *Montana Dream, Life on the Montana Frontier, Montana to Boston and Back, Montana Sons Go to War,* and *Montana Sons Return from War.* The Donaldson series of two novels is available: *Rite of Passage* and *Rite of Marriage.*

This is a link to Barbara's website to view all of her books http://barbararaue.ca

www.ingramcontent.com/pod-product-compliance
Lightning Source LLC
Chambersburg PA
CBHW041941240526
45473CB00033B/192